THE
SON OF SAM
KILLINGS

By Alexis Burling

CONTENT CONSULTANT

JOSEPH CILLO, JD
ASSISTANT PROFESSOR, CRIMINAL JUSTICE
SAINT LEO UNIVERSITY

AMERICAN
CRIME
STORIES

Essential Library

An Imprint of Abdo Publishing | abdobooks.com

ABDOBOOKS.COM

Published by Abdo Publishing, a division of ABDO, PO Box 398166, Minneapolis, Minnesota 55439. Copyright © 2020 by Abdo Consulting Group, Inc. International copyrights reserved in all countries. No part of this book may be reproduced in any form without written permission from the publisher. Essential Library™ is a trademark and logo of Abdo Publishing.

Printed in the United States of America, North Mankato, Minnesota.
102019
012020

Cover Photo: AP Images
Interior Photos: Jerry Engel/New York Post Archives/Getty Images, 5; New York Daily News Archive/Getty Images, 6, 17, 22, 29, 67; AP Images, 7, 15, 25, 26, 36, 37, 45, 50, 65, 74–75; Red Line Editorial, 12, 60; Charles Frattini/New York Daily News Archive/Getty Images, 33; Rainer Lesniewski/Shutterstock Images, 38; Richard Lee/New York Post Archives/Getty Images, 41; Ron Frehm/AP Images, 43; Ira Schwartz/AP Images, 46; Jim Varney/Science Source, 53; Ira Schwartz/AP Images, 55; Stephen Shames/Polaris/Newscom, 59; Jack Smith/New York Daily News Archive/Getty Images, 62–63; Dan Goodrich/AP Images, 70; Allan Tannenbaum/Polaris/Newscom, 77; Spencer A. Burnett/New York Post Archives/Getty Images, 81; iStockphoto, 84; Frederick M. Brown/Getty Images Entertainment/Getty Images, 87; CBS News/AP Images, 92; NC1/WENN/Newscom, 96–97

Editor: Charly Haley
Series Designer: Melissa Martin

LIBRARY OF CONGRESS CONTROL NUMBER: 2019942069

PUBLISHER'S CATALOGING-IN-PUBLICATION DATA

Names: Burling, Alexis, author.
Title: The Son of Sam killings / by Alexis Burling
Description: Minneapolis, Minnesota : Abdo Publishing, 2020 | Series: American crime stories | Includes online resources and index.
Identifiers: ISBN 9781532190148 (lib. bdg) | ISBN 9781532175992 (ebook)
Subjects: LCSH: Son of Sam, 1953- (David Berkowitz)--Juvenile literature. | Serial killers--Juvenile literature. | Killing (Murder)--Juvenile literature. | Homicide--Juvenile literature. | Murder--New York (State)--New York--Juvenile literature.
Classification: DDC 364.152--dc23

CONTENTS

CHAPTER ONE

SHOTS IN THE DARK

I t was just after 1:00 a.m. in muggy New York City on July 29, 1976. Eighteen-year-old Donna Lauria and her close friend, 19-year-old Jody Valenti, had just arrived home after a night of dancing at a disco in New Rochelle, a nearby suburb. They were sitting in Valenti's Oldsmobile Cutlass, parked outside Lauria's family's apartment in the Bronx, getting in some last-minute chitchat before saying goodbye for the night.

Lauria glanced at the clock and noticed the late hour. She reached for the car door handle when suddenly, a dark shadow appeared. A man in a striped shirt approached the car. He reached into the brown paper bag he was holding and took out a gun. Before the teenagers had time to register what was going on, the man fired at least four rounds into the car.

Lauria and Valenti were in this corner of the Bronx when they were attacked by an unknown man with a gun.

Donna Lauria

A bullet slammed into Lauria's back. She fell out of the car and lay sprawled out on the pavement. Valenti shrieked as a bullet struck her thigh. She fell forward from the shock, banging her head on the car's horn.

Lauria's father, Michael, heard the noise from his living room. He ran outside to see what the commotion was and found his dying daughter on the ground, bleeding profusely. Valenti was still inside the car, screaming. The person who committed the crime had vanished.

"I ran down, by the time I got down, she was dead in the street," Michael Lauria later told *CBS News*. "My daughter was 18 years old and that's what [her murderer] took out of my heart, 18 years."[1] Donna Lauria was taken away in an

DONNA LAURIA (1957–1976)

Many people remembered Donna Lauria as a bright young woman with a promising future. She had trained for two years as an emergency medical technician for the Empire State Ambulance Service at New York Hospital and was well-loved by her colleagues. She had a lot in common with her friend Jody Valenti, who lived nearby on Hutchinson River Parkway and was studying to become a nurse.

Lauria was the middle child and only daughter of Rose and Michael Lauria. In 2016, 40 years after her daughter was killed, Rose Lauria was interviewed by PIX11, a local TV station. She and her husband had just celebrated their sixty-third wedding anniversary. They had four grandchildren, including one who they said looked just like their deceased daughter. Rose told PIX11 that she was thankful for her family. Still, she held on to what had happened to her daughter. "I'm a changed person," she told PIX11. "[But] there's not a day that goes by [Donna's] not on my mind."[2]

ambulance, but there was nothing the medics could do. Valenti, still distraught, was driven to a nearby hospital and treated for her wounds. When she had calmed down enough to speak, officers from the New York City Police Department (NYPD) tried to get a statement from her about what happened.

Unpromising Leads

The gruesome attack deeply traumatized Valenti. But when the police asked her if she had any idea who might have tried to kill her and her close friend, she couldn't come up with a name. She didn't have any enemies. As far as she knew, none of Lauria's ex-boyfriends were the type to commit such a violent act.

Valenti later gave detectives a sparse description of the killer so they could create a composite sketch. The shooter was definitely a man. Though Valenti wasn't 100 percent sure,

LONG-LASTING FEAR

Although Jody Valenti survived the shooting on the night of July 29, 1976, she was haunted for decades by the moment when a gunman shot her and her friend Donna Lauria at close range. It took her 40 years to speak publicly about what happened that night. In a July 2016 *New York Post* article, Valenti said she had suffered from ongoing post-traumatic stress. She couldn't get in a car at night for more than five years after the incident. Loud noises terrified her. Valenti said she didn't think she'd ever buy a gun herself. But after a mass shooting in Newton, Connecticut, in 2012, Valenti took a class to face her fears. "I went and learned how to shoot a gun," she told the *Post*. "I did it to face my fear of a gun, my fear of holding a gun . . . my fear of the sound of a gun—fear, fear, fear."[3]

A MAFIA HIT?

In the 1970s, both Lauria and Valenti lived in an area of New York City called the Bronx. It's one of the area's five boroughs, located north of Manhattan. The North Bronx is populated by many different cultural groups, including Italian Americans. The area was also a hotbed for the Mafia, an Italian American organized crime network with operations in cities across the United States.

Lauria was murdered outside a six-story apartment building at 2860 Buhre Avenue, an affluent Italian American area where the Mafia was known to operate. Because of this location, some people, including the police, jumped to the conclusion that the shooting must have been perpetrated by a member of the Mafia. "That's the [Mafia]," said former NYPD Detective Sergeant Joseph Coffey. "The wise guys, they whack people, shoot them in the head."[4] However, in later months, as new details about the nature of the crime materialized, the Mafia theory was discarded.

she guessed he was around 30 years old and white. She also mentioned that he had dark, curly hair.

As with any homicide case, the NYPD interviewed any neighbors they could find who could verify Valenti's description or who might have witnessed something else related to the crime. A few people reported seeing a yellow car parked a few cars behind Valenti's that night, but it was gone by the time the police arrived on the scene. With hardly any leads, police believed the

According to experts' estimates, hand-drawn sketches by trained artists are only about 9 percent accurate in producing a recognizable likeness to a suspect; computer-generated drawings are only 5 percent accurate.[5]

9

shooting was simply another occurrence of bizarre, random violence during a fraught period in New York City when drug use and homicides were on the rise. Serious crime was at an all-time high in the city—six times higher than the national average.[6] The murder of Lauria barely got a mention in the press.

Summer of Fear

Unbeknownst to anyone at the time, David Berkowitz—the man who had committed the brutal attack—would evade capture for more than a year. He would strike again. And again. And again. In total, he would kill six people and injure seven more before being caught and arrested in August 1977.[7]

Berkowitz's premeditated murders were shocking and unpredictable. But they did not seem entirely unconnected—the murders had many things in common with one

A PREVIOUS ATTACK

Once it became clear they were dealing with a serial killer, NYPD detectives assumed the shooting of Lauria and Valenti was the killer's first attack. It didn't become clear until much later that this violent man had struck before. On December 24, 1975, David Berkowitz stabbed two women using a hunting knife. Michelle Forman was only 15 years old, and she was severely wounded in the attack. The other victim was slightly injured and escaped quickly. She has never been identified.

David Berkowitz

another. The victims were young and attractive. Most were couples seated in parked cars in the early hours of the morning. Many of the women who were attacked had dark hair. Each of the killings took place in the boroughs of New York City, some within blocks of each other. All of the attacks instilled fear in

SON OF SAM STATS

5 of the shootings occurred in Queens; **2** happened in the Bronx; **2** took place in Brooklyn.

9 of the victims were women and **4** were men.

7 of the victims were teenagers; **5** were 20 years old; **1** was 26.

4 of the couples had been to the movies before being shot by Berkowitz.[8]

the hearts and minds of people all over the city and across the nation.

The homicides also confounded the police. In the 13 months between Berkowitz's first murder and the moment he was finally caught, detectives in precincts up and down New York City struggled for answers as to who the serial killer might be. They interviewed dozens of promising eyewitnesses, only to wind up at dead ends.

David Berkowitz, also referred to as the Son of Sam, became one of the most notorious criminals in the United States. To this day, he is still considered one of the most disturbing and frightening figures of all time. As is the case with many serial killers, some historians say there were clues early on in Berkowitz's concerning childhood behaviors. But no one, not even Berkowitz himself, had any inkling of the killer he would become.

CHAPTER TWO

A TROUBLED PAST

Berkowitz was born Richard David Falco on June 1, 1953, in Brooklyn, New York. Betty Falco, his birth mother, was an aspiring Broadway dancer. She was unmarried, poor, and unable to take care of a newborn baby, so she put her son up for adoption. Nathan and Pearl Berkowitz, a Jewish couple living in the Bronx, adopted the boy when he was just a few days old. Rather than giving him an entirely new name, they reversed his first and middle names, calling him David Richard Berkowitz.

The Berkowitzes raised their son in a one-bedroom apartment. They lived a relatively simple life. Nathan Berkowitz owned a hardware store. When Berkowitz was a child, he was close with his adoptive parents, especially his mother. As he grew older, however, he became introverted and sullen. Though he was smart, he didn't do well in school. He frequently got in trouble for stealing from local shops. He also loved to

Berkowitz grew up in the Bronx, a New York City neighborhood where he would later shoot and kill multiple people.

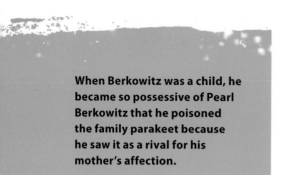

set small fires around the neighborhood but never got caught.

When Berkowitz was a child, he became so possessive of Pearl Berkowitz that he poisoned the family parakeet because he saw it as a rival for his mother's affection.

In 1967, when Berkowitz was 14, Pearl Berkowitz died from breast cancer. The loss of his mother sent the already-troubled teenager into a tailspin. "I loved her very much," he later told Dr. David Abrahamsen, a psychiatrist from Columbia University. "After Mother's death, I lost the capacity to love."[1]

To make matters worse, Berkowitz's father soon remarried. Berkowitz didn't get along with his new stepmother and became even more of a loner. In 1971, when he turned 18, he joined the US Army and was eventually sent to South Korea. It was there that Berkowitz first shot a gun. He served as one of his company's sharpshooters.

Warning Signs

After two years of service in the United States and a year in South Korea, Berkowitz was honorably discharged from the army in 1974. He returned to New York and moved into an apartment at 2161 Barnes Avenue in the Bronx. He cycled in and out of blue-collar jobs, including as an unarmed security guard and a US postal worker. During this time, his bad moods grew

Beginning at age 18, Berkowitz served in the US Army for about three years.

severe. He didn't have many friends. Though he wanted to date, he never had anything close to a serious romantic relationship. In letters to his father, who had moved with his new wife to Florida, Berkowitz often rambled about his fragile mental state.

"It's cold and gloomy here in New York, but that's okay because the weather fits my mood—gloomy. Dad, the world is getting dark now. I can feel it more and more," he wrote. "The people, they are developing a hatred for me. You wouldn't believe how much some people hate me. Many of them want to kill me. I don't even know these people, but they still hate me. Most of them are young. I walk down the street and they spit and kick at me. The girls call me ugly and they bother me the most."[2]

In an attempt to give his life some sort of meaning, Berkowitz embarked on a search for his birth mother in 1975. He found her in Queens, one of New York City's five boroughs. On Mother's Day, he dropped a card in her mailbox. Betty Falco was intrigued by the possibility of reuniting with the son she had given up for adoption years ago. She welcomed "Richie" into her life.

The amicable feelings didn't last long, however. After meeting his half-sister, Berkowitz became angered by the idea that he had a sibling Falco had kept while he had been discarded. He also found out that his birth father was a married man with whom Falco had had a longtime affair, an

RAGE AND FIRE

After Berkowitz returned from serving in South Korea, he was still distraught over his adoptive mother's death. In an attempt to lash out, he quickly reignited his pyromania-like tendencies and started setting fires around New York City and its suburbs. Over the course of three years, Berkowitz set as many as 2,000 fires.[3] The police only found out about his role in the blazes after he was arrested in 1977 in connection with the murders. The cops found meticulously detailed records in his apartment, documenting where and when the fires had happened. He was never prosecuted for these crimes.

act Berkowitz found disrespectful and disgusting. Though he continued to visit Falco, he distanced himself from her emotionally. He also made the decision to close himself off from the rest of the world, especially women, as much as possible.

"I was filled with anger and rage toward Betty. I was getting a very powerful urge to kill most of my 'natural' family," Berkowitz later told Abrahamsen. "I want to be a lover to women, but I want to destroy them too. Especially women who dance. Them I hate. I hate their sensuality, their moral laxity. I'm no saint myself but I blame them for everything."[4]

A Gruesome Attack

By the end of 1975, Berkowitz had reached a breaking point. He had started hearing voices in his mind that prompted him to do evil deeds. On Christmas Eve, he decided to take action. He grabbed a hunting knife with a four-and-a-half-inch blade and drove to a supermarket in Co-Op City, a towering block of apartment buildings on the edge of the Bronx where he and his adoptive father had lived after Pearl Berkowitz's death. He saw a woman walking alone, carrying a bag of groceries. Without second-guessing his motives, he took out the knife and stabbed the woman.

"She was screaming pitifully and I didn't know what the hell to do," Berkowitz later said in an interview. "It wasn't like the movies. In the movies you sneak up on someone and they fall

SELF-INDUCED ISOLATION

In late November 1975, Berkowitz took some time off from his job as a security guard for IBI Armored Services. He had been working the night shift providing security at a trucking company near John F. Kennedy International Airport, and he felt he needed a break from the monotony of the job. But instead of being rejuvenating, the vacation was isolating.

Berkowitz spent 28 days alone in his apartment, leaving only to buy food and soda from the grocery store. He nailed sheets over the windows to block out the daylight. According to records from his journals, he scrawled tormented notes on the bare walls. One read, "In this hole lives the Wicked King. Kill for my master."[6] At the end of the 28-day stint, Berkowitz went out and stabbed Michelle Forman and an unidentified woman.

down quietly, dead. It wasn't like that. She was staring at my knife and screaming. She wasn't dying."[5]

Scared by the noise and fearful he would be discovered, Berkowitz ran away to find another victim. As he neared a pedestrian bridge that crossed over the New York State Thruway, he spotted 15-year-old Michelle Forman, a sophomore at Truman High School. He stabbed her six times in the back of her head and throughout her body. She, too, fought off Berkowitz's attack and shrieked as loud as she could. Though she was severely injured, she survived.

Berkowitz fled the scene of the crime, unscathed. About a month later, in February 1976, the 22-year-old moved to an apartment in a two-family home in New Rochelle, a working-class suburb of New York City. The voices in his head got worse. This time, they took the form of barks from the neighborhood dogs, including his landlord's German shepherd next door. Berkowitz believed that the barks he heard told him to murder attractive young girls. "The demons never stopped. I couldn't sleep. I had no strength to fight. I could barely drive," he later wrote in his journals. "Coming home from work one night, I almost killed myself in the car. I needed to sleep. . . . The demons wouldn't give me any peace."[7]

After Berkowitz stabbed the unknown woman and Michelle Forman on December 24, 1975, he reportedly drove to a nearby all-night diner and ordered a burger and fries.

Berkowitz became so disturbed by the barking that he moved to an apartment on Pine Street in Yonkers not even three months later. Again, the voices—or barks—intensified. Harvey, a black Labrador retriever owned by Berkowitz's neighbor, Sam Carr, was particularly irritating to Berkowitz. That May, Berkowitz drove down to Texas to visit an old friend from the army. He also got a gun. In just a few months, he would use it for the first time.

Serial Killings

Late on the night of July 28, 1976, Berkowitz walked up to a car in the Bronx and shot two women. He fired multiple times with his .44-caliber revolver. Eighteen-year-old Donna Lauria was killed instantly. Her friend, Jody Valenti, was wounded. The murder went unsolved by the police. So, Berkowitz struck again.

On October 23, 1976, Berkowitz shot at 18-year-old Rosemary Keenan and her boyfriend, Carl Denaro, a 20-year-old bank security guard, while they were sitting in Denaro's parked car in Flushing, Queens. Both survived, but one of the bullets

Sam Carr, *left*, with his dog, Harvey, and his daughter. It's believed that Berkowitz drew the name "Son of Sam" from the first name of his neighbor, Carr.

struck Denaro's head. He had to have a steel plate placed inside his skull to prevent swelling.

About a month later, Berkowitz tried to kill again. On November 27, 1976, he shot 17-year-old Donna DeMasi and 18-year-old Joanne Lomino as they were sitting on Lomino's porch in Bellerose, Queens. They had just returned from a late-night movie in Manhattan when Berkowitz came up to them, asking for directions. He then pulled out his revolver and shot them. DeMasi survived without suffering permanent physical damage, but Lomino was paralyzed from her waist down when a bullet struck her spine. The police found three shell casings at the scene, but the evidence didn't lead to any arrests.

After these two shootings, which resulted in no deaths, Berkowitz tried once more to kill. At 12:30 a.m. on January 30, 1977, he saw two people sitting in a parked red Pontiac Firebird outside the Long Island Rail Road Station in Forest Hills, Queens.

SERIAL KILLER STATISTICS

Serial killers like Berkowitz are rare. As reported in the *Scientific American*, serial killings account for no more than 1 percent of all murders committed in the United States.[8] According to the Federal Bureau of Investigation (FBI), there are between 25 and 50 serial killers operating throughout the country at any given point.[9] The FBI also states that, contrary to popular belief, these murderers are not all loner misfits. Many are educated, married, and employed. Serial killers can be any gender and belong to any racial group.

The couple—26-year-old Christine Freund and her fiancé, 30-year-old John Diel—had just seen the movie Rocky and were planning to go dancing. Then Berkowitz approached with a gun. He fired three shots, killing Freund. Diel survived the attack.

By this time, people throughout New York City were on edge. Though the city was filled with crime, the fact that young people kept getting shot in the safe space of their cars was particularly unnerving. The police were growing more suspicious, too. Though they suspected the crimes were linked by the same .44 gun, they didn't have concrete evidence to prove it. They also couldn't pin down a motive.

Then, on March 8, 1977, everything changed. Nineteen-year-old Columbia University student Virginia Voskerichian was shot in her mouth at close range in

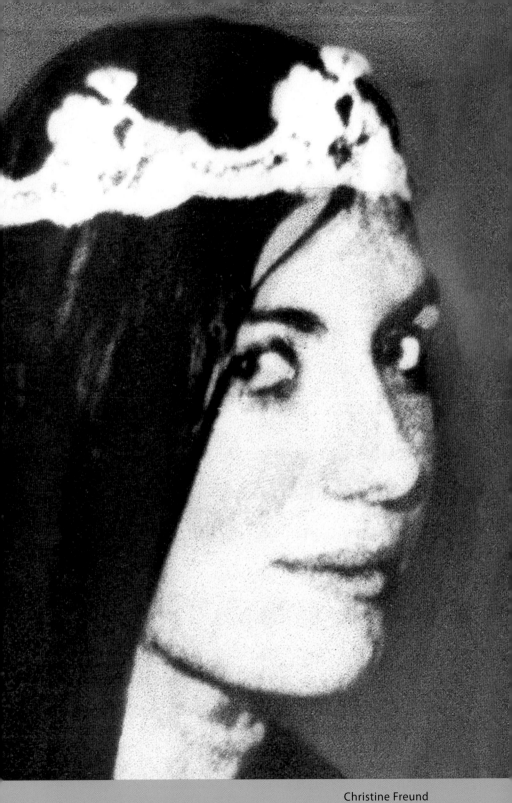

Christine Freund

Virginia Voskerichian

Forest Hills, Queens, as she was walking home. She lived a block away from Christine Freund. When the cops arrived, they found Voskerichian facedown on the sidewalk. She died at the scene.

As police investigated the area, they discovered a bullet in the bushes, linking Voskerichian's murder to the gun used in Lauria's death. It was a turning point in the case. A witness also saw a dark-haired white man who looked about 18 years old, average height and build, running away right after the murder happened. He was reportedly wearing dark clothes, a ski hat, and a waist-length jacket. This description was similar to the way Valenti had described her attacker to investigators. The next day, the NYPD held a press conference to explain to the media what they had discovered. The police now knew the incidents weren't isolated or perpetrated by multiple, unrelated killers. Instead, they were the work of a serial killer who would most likely strike again unless he was caught.

A BULLET'S IDENTITY

In many cases, detectives and police are able to solve a crime by connecting a bullet found at a crime scene to the gun that fired it. But how does that happen? When a gun is fired, a bullet explodes down the gun's barrel. Along the way, the bullet scrapes up against unique ridges and grooves in the gun's barrel that cause it to spin. These ridges leave markings on the bullet, which is made of soft metal. The marks are unique and can be linked to a specific gun. When police try to solve a crime, they often examine a suspect's gun and any bullets they find at the scene of the crime. If the marks on the bullets and the suspect's gun barrel match, the suspect is most likely the one who pulled the trigger.

CHAPTER THREE

THE SUMMER
OF SAM

On the morning of April 18, 1977, New Yorkers woke up to find a chilling headline in the *New York Daily News*: ".44-Cal Slayer Kills Girl, Beau."[1] The city's serial killer had struck again, this time killing both of his victims. The circumstances of their deaths were frighteningly familiar.

Eighteen-year-old Valentina Suriani, an acting major at Lehman College in the Bronx, was sitting in a brown Mercury Montego with her boyfriend, 20-year-old Alexander Esau. It was 3:00 a.m., and they had just returned from a late-night movie. The car was parked on a quiet street near Suriani's home on Hutchinson River Parkway in the Bronx, just a few blocks from where Donna Lauria and Jody Valenti had been shot.

Without warning, the killer approached the driver's side window and fired a few rounds into the car. Suriani was killed

Before Berkowitz became known as the Son of Sam, the media often called him the ".44 Killer" or variations of that name, which referred to the type of gun used in the shootings.

44-CAL SLAYER
KILLS GIRL, BEAU

un Linked to 3 Other Deaths

News photo
alentina Suriani, 18, and Alexander Esau, 20, were killed by gunman in the Bronx.
Story on page 3

14% Pay Hike
Averts Strike
Against State
Page 2

Rabin's Wife
Is Fined 26G
Page 2

Speak Out
**Taxes—How Would
You Change Them?**
Page 5

DEMONIC SPIRITS

The note left after the murder on April 17, 1977, was the first time David Berkowitz identified himself using the name "Son of Sam." Some historians suggest Berkowitz used the name in reference to his Yonkers neighbor, Sam Carr, and Carr's dog, Harvey. Berkowitz believed the dog and its master were demonic spirits who were urging him to stalk and kill women.

The day after the Suriani and Esau slayings, the *Daily News* ran a story about the note, exclaiming that its author was a "homicidal maniac."[3] An unnamed source from the NYPD was quoted as saying the killer's calling card "came close to giving clues, but in a rambling, almost incomprehensible style" and that he "lives in a nightmare world where he sees blood-sucking vampires and Frankenstein monsters."[4] The note was later taken to the NYPD's crime lab to be analyzed by fingerprint and handwriting experts.

instantly. Esau was hit in his head by two bullets. He later died at nearby Jacobi Medical Center.

When the police arrived on the scene, they noticed similarities to some of the other murders that had taken place in and around the Bronx and Queens over the previous few months. The victims were young and sitting in a parked car. The bullets that killed them were from the same type of gun used in previous slayings, a .44-caliber revolver. But there was also a striking addition to this crime scene. The killer had left a handwritten note addressed to Joseph Borrelli, the captain of the NYPD Queens homicide unit. In it, he promised the cops that he'd kill again. "Police—Let me haunt you with these words: I'll be back! I'll be back! To be interpreted as—Bang, Bang, Bang, Bang, Bang—UGH!! Yours In Murder," the note said.[2] The killer signed the letter "Son of Sam."

Suspicions Build

The fact that Berkowitz had claimed his third and fourth victims in an uncannily similar manner reinforced the NYPD's belief that they were dealing with a serial murderer. The police department formed a task force of 50 detectives whose sole focus was to find out who the Son of Sam was and track him down. It was called Operation Omega, led by Manhattan-based deputy inspector Timothy Dowd. They set up a tip phone line just for Son of Sam leads.

Meanwhile, as the largest manhunt in New York City's history up until that time got underway, seemingly unrelated developments took place in Yonkers. Some of the residents of the Pine Hill Towers had noticed their relatively new neighbor's strange behavior. On April 29, someone shot and nearly killed

TIMOTHY DOWD

Timothy Dowd was born on May 30, 1915, in County Kerry, Ireland. His parents were originally farmers, but they relocated the family to the United States during the Great Depression, eventually settling in New York. Dowd attended City College of New York and got a master's degree from Baruch College. When he was 25, he joined the police force. A year later, in 1941, he married his wife, Helen Cavanaugh. The couple had a daughter and three sons.

Dowd started as a member of the NYPD unit of officers who patrol on horseback. But he soon advanced to become a detective in homicide and narcotics. Because of his success as a lead detective on the Son of Sam case, Dowd received a rare promotion of two ranks, from deputy inspector to deputy chief. A year after Berkowitz's conviction, Dowd retired. He died on December 26, 2014, at the age of 99.

Harvey, Sam Carr's dog. Though no one could prove Berkowitz was the perpetrator, a nasty anonymous letter sent to Carr about the dog's barking seemed to point in Berkowitz's direction. Berkowitz had also started sending unusual letters to other neighbors, complaining about noise and ranting about satanic forces taking over the world. Some of the residents in Berkowitz's building—including Craig Glassman, a volunteer deputy sheriff who lived directly below Berkowitz—suspected there was something wrong with him and reported their concerns to local police.

Special Deputy Sheriff Craig Glassman filed a harassment complaint against his neighbor David Berkowitz on August 6, 1977. Glassman believed Berkowitz was responsible for setting a fire outside his apartment door that contained live bullets. At the time, Glassman didn't know that Berkowitz was a serial killer.

Citywide Panic

Then, on May 30, 1977, after a month of no public activity, the Son of Sam sent a note to *New York Daily News* newspaper columnist Jimmy Breslin. It was postmarked from Englewood, New Jersey. The envelope had the words "Blood and Family— Darkness and Death—Absolute Depravity—.44" written on the outside.[5] The letter referenced some of the Son of Sam's past victims. It also mocked the NYPD for its failure to crack the case.

People across New York City became fearful as the Son of Sam killings continued. They wondered who the mysterious killer was and whom he could target next.

The note read, in part, "Hello from the gutters of NYC which are filled with dog manure, vomit, stale wine, urine, and blood. Hello from the sewers of NYC which swallow up these delicacies when they are washed away by the sweeper trucks. . . . J.B., I'm just dropping you a line to let you know that I appreciate your interest in those recent and horrendous .44 [caliber] killings."[6]

The *Daily News* printed the Son of Sam's note to Breslin a few days later. It set off a citywide panic that lasted for months and prompted New Yorkers to start calling this time period the "Summer of Sam." Many young people, especially women, avoided walking alone late at night. "I'm afraid. I'm afraid to go out in the car. I'm afraid to do anything. You never know where he's going to be," one woman said in an interview.[7]

Another woman said, "You have to be careful. You have to watch where you go now, how late you stay out and who you talk to. I'm always with someone. I know I'm going to be taken right home. . . . It scares you."[8] Some women stopped going out altogether for fear of becoming the next victim.

Another Shooting

On June 26 at 3:20 a.m., Berkowitz shot a couple as they were sitting in a maroon Cadillac Coupe de Ville a block away from the Eléphas disco in Bayside, Queens. Seventeen-year-old Judy Placido was shot in her right temple, her right shoulder, and the back of her neck. Her date, 20-year-old Salvatore Lupo, was shot in his right forearm. Both survived, but they were clearly shaken.

Son of Sam victims Judy Placido and Valentina Suriani both graduated from St. Catharine Academy, a high school in the Bronx, a year apart.

Still bleeding from his wounds, Lupo stumbled back to the disco to get help. People at the club tried for 15 minutes to call 911, but the number was jammed. Two people, one of whom was an off-duty police officer, ran three blocks to the Bayside police station to report the shooting. According to an article in the *Daily News*, an unidentified man had called the station the week prior. "This is Son of Sam," he had said to the officer who answered the phone. "Next week I'm going to hit Bayside."[9] At the time of that call, it was considered just another potential lead on top of dozens of others the cops had to investigate.

A Major Breakthrough

By July 1977, a year had passed since the Son of Sam's first murder. Though Operation Omega was in full swing, the NYPD wasn't any closer to pinning down the serial killer's identity. Afraid of being this unknown killer's next victims, people stayed away from parties and late-night meals, causing restaurants and bars to lose money. New Yorkers were also weathering an unbearable heat wave. Temperatures reached more than 100 degrees Fahrenheit (37.7°C).[10]

At about 2:50 a.m. on July 31, two days after the one-year anniversary of Donna Lauria's death, the Son of Sam shot a couple sitting in a brown Buick in Brooklyn. Twenty-year-old

A DARK TIME IN NYC

July 13, 1977, was a memorable day in New York City's history for many reasons. The Son of Sam had already brutally murdered five people. The cops didn't have enough strong leads to pin down a suspect. Temperatures were unbearably hot. Crime was on the rise. Then, at 9:34 p.m., lightning hit. All the lights across the five boroughs went out. The city plunged into darkness. By the time the lights came back on 25 hours later, thieves had looted 1,600 stores, and arsonists had set more than 1,000 fires. As a result, more than 3,700 people were arrested. New York City officials estimated that the blackout cost more than $300 million. It was a terrifying time in New York. "The Son of Sam thing had every woman in New York freaked," one New Yorker remembers. "Everyone looked at everyone sideways."[11]

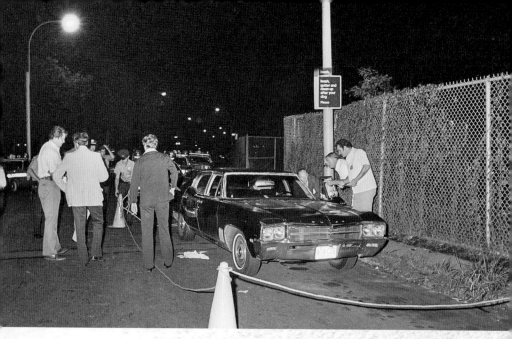

Police investigate the area where the Son of Sam shot Moskowitz and Violante.

Stacy Moskowitz, a secretary, and 20-year-old Robert Violante, a clothing store salesman, were on their first date. They had seen *New York, New York* at a local movie theater and had gone to Jasmines, a disco in Bay Ridge. Then they stopped by Dyker Beach Park in Bensonhurst on their way home. Neither of them saw the gunman approach. As in previous attacks, he crouched down, aimed at the car window, and fired multiple rounds. Both Moskowitz and Violante were shot in the head. Witnesses reported Violante banged on the car horn, fell out of the car, and yelled, "Help me! Don't let me die!"[12] Moskowitz died at Kings County Hospital. Violante survived, but he lost most of his eyesight.

After the shooting, the Son of Sam put the gun away, turned around, and calmly crossed the street into a nearby park. He may have thought he got away that night unnoticed. But Tommy Zaino, who just happened to be parked behind the slain couple, got a good look at the shooter. Zaino told the police that the assailant was a stocky white man between 25 and 35 years old. He was wearing a light-colored shirt with rolled-up sleeves and jeans.

Another witness proved to be even more helpful. Cacilia Davis was out late walking her dog, Snowball, when she passed

Stacy Moskowitz

WHERE DID
BERKOWITZ ATTACK?

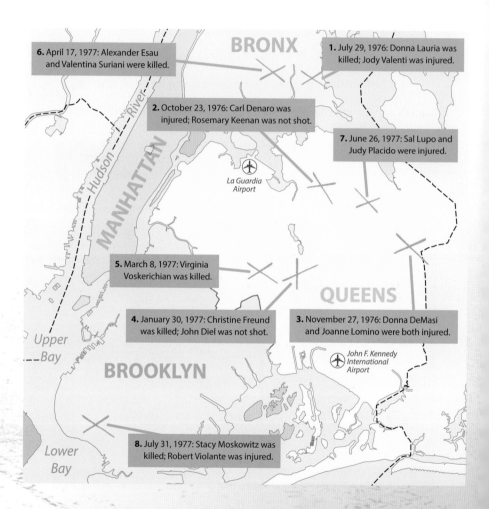

6. April 17, 1977: Alexander Esau and Valentina Suriani were killed.

BRONX

1. July 29, 1976: Donna Lauria was killed; Jody Valenti was injured.

2. October 23, 1976: Carl Denaro was injured; Rosemary Keenan was not shot.

7. June 26, 1977: Sal Lupo and Judy Placido were injured.

Hudson River

MANHATTAN

La Guardia Airport

5. March 8, 1977: Virginia Voskerichian was killed.

QUEENS

4. January 30, 1977: Christine Freund was killed; John Diel was not shot.

3. November 27, 1976: Donna DeMasi and Joanne Lomino were both injured.

Upper Bay

John F. Kennedy International Airport

BROOKLYN

8. July 31, 1977: Stacy Moskowitz was killed; Robert Violante was injured.

Lower Bay

David Berkowitz shot people eight times throughout Queens, the Bronx, and Brooklyn. He killed six people and wounded seven.

a "nice fellow" on the street. "He was so obvious. It was hot, and he had a shirt and a jacket on, and he walked with his right arm straight down," Davis later told the police. "I could see he was holding something, but from the front I couldn't tell what it was. As he walked away, I could see it was something he had partly up his sleeve."[13]

Davis also remembered seeing police officer Michael Cataneo doling out parking tickets near her apartment, which was close to where the shooting had happened. One of the ticketed cars was parked too close to a fire hydrant. When Davis called her local police station a few days later to report what she had seen, they sent a detective and a sketch artist over to her apartment to sort out the details. The cops also ran the license plates on the cars that had received parking tickets in the area. One of the cars, a Ford Galaxy, was registered as belonging to David Berkowitz.

Based on Berkowitz's Yonkers address, Detective James Justus called the Yonkers Police Department to see if they knew anything about Berkowitz. After all, Justus remembers thinking, what was a guy from Yonkers doing down in that neighborhood at that time of night? "This has got to be the guy. This has got to be the guy," he said to the Yonkers dispatcher, who just happened to be Wheat Carr, Sam Carr's daughter. "I can't put my finger on it. Something's wrong with this."[14] Little did Justus know how close he was to catching the elusive serial killer.

CHAPTER FOUR

CAPTURED

By early August 1977, the Son of Sam had murdered six people and wounded seven others. Police all over New York City were on high alert for anything that looked suspicious, especially in the Bronx and Queens, where most of the shootings had happened. More than 100 additional officers were assigned to the case after the attack on Moskowitz and Violante, bringing the total to 300.[1] New Yorkers were fearful, and tensions continued to escalate.

"If terrorists might well pose a greater potential danger to more people, there was much more apprehension of the threat of random shots in the dark from the lone gunman," a *Time* magazine reporter wrote at the time. "[The Son of Sam] has haunted lovers' lanes, attacked couples coming from strobe-lighted discotheques, even opened fire at a pair of girls on a house porch and shot another as he passed her on a street."[2]

A street vendor sells a newspaper featuring the Son of Sam on the front page in August 1977.

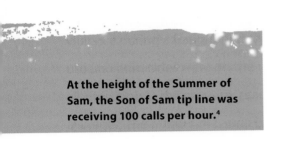

At the height of the Summer of Sam, the Son of Sam tip line was receiving 100 calls per hour.[4]

Calls flooded in to police stations across New York City and to the Son of Sam tip line. Women called in about their husbands, ex-boyfriends, and coworkers. Though some of the callers corroborated previous descriptions of the person who might have been the killer— white man, dark hair, stocky build, mid-20s—others offered new details that didn't add up. Many police officers working on the case expressed frustration with the lack of progress and with the number of callers falsely claiming to be the Son of Sam. "He's given himself up 12 times already today," a detective taking calls from the Son of Sam line later told the *Daily News*.[3]

Despite the setbacks, the investigation finally began to move forward in the days following Moskowitz's death. On August 3, as a result of eyewitness statements from Davis and Zaino, police released a new Son of Sam sketch to the media. With the help of Sergeant Mike Novotny and other detectives at the Yonkers Police Department, the NYPD traced the parking ticket to David Berkowitz's car registered at 35 Pine Street, the Pine Hill Towers. At the time, detectives thought 24-year-old Berkowitz might have been a witness to the shooting of Moskowitz and Violante. But they would soon find out he was much more than that.

The Pine Hill Towers apartments, where Berkowitz lived, shown in 1977

Arresting Berkowitz

On August 10, a team of officers, including homicide detectives Edward Zigo and John Falotico, went to the Pine Hill Towers, hoping to interview Berkowitz about what he might have seen on July 31. But when they found his car and looked into its windows, they immediately changed their minds and switched tactics. Through the car's window, officers saw a letter sitting on the front seat, written in the Son of Sam's familiar handwriting. The officers spotted a duffel bag and a large machine gun in the back seat, too. A .44-caliber revolver was also clearly visible in the car. Not wanting to blow their cover, the officers went back to their car and waited for Berkowitz to emerge from the apartment building.

A few moments later, Berkowitz came out of his apartment and got into his car. When Detective Falotico ordered him to step out of the vehicle, Berkowitz didn't struggle or resist arrest. Instead, he said, "Well, you've got me."[5] He also asked the officers what had taken them so long.

After arresting Berkowitz, officers rushed him from Yonkers to the NYPD headquarters. At 1:40 a.m. on August 11, New York City Mayor Abraham Beame held a press conference in lower Manhattan. "I am very pleased to announce that the people of the City of New York can rest easy tonight because police have captured a man they believe to be the Son of Sam," Beame said.[6] The event brought an end to one of the most chaotic and distressing periods in New York City history.

ANOTHER NONSENSICAL NOTE

When detectives Edward Zigo and John Falotico searched Berkowitz's car on the night of his arrest, they found weapons, ammunition, and maps of the crime scenes. There was also one of the Son of Sam's signature letters addressed to Detective Dowd. In Berkowitz's chicken-scratch handwriting, some of the seemingly nonsensical note read as follows: "Because Craig is Craig so must the streets be filled with crime (death) and huge drops of lead poured down upon her head until she was dead. Yet the cats still come out at night to mate and the sparrows still sing in the morning."[7]

A Speedy Trial

The day after Berkowitz's arrest, he willingly confessed to the murders of five women and one

Several police officers were involved in arresting Berkowitz outside of his apartment on August 10, 1977.

After Berkowitz's arrest, New York City officials and the NYPD held a press conference to share the news.

man, and the maiming of at least seven other people. He claimed he would plead guilty to any charges brought against him. When asked for his motives, Berkowitz replied that his neighbor, 64-year-old Sam Carr, "really [was] a man who lived 6,000 years ago" and who "told [him] to kill"[8] by speaking through his dog. Obviously, this was not true. Berkowitz also recounted the excruciating details of each of his crimes.

"When they talked to David Berkowitz that night, he recalled everything step by step by step, the guy has

1000 percent recall and that's it," reported Jimmy Breslin. "He's the guy and there's nothing else to look at."[9]

After Berkowitz's confession, he was sent to Kings County Hospital for a psychiatric evaluation, the

After Berkowitz was arrested and had confessed to the Son of Sam killings, 25 officers were promoted because of their work on the case. It was the largest number of promotions related to a single case in NYPD history.[11]

same hospital where Moskowitz had died just a few days earlier. Though doctors agreed that his ramblings were strange, they believed he was competent to stand trial. Berkowitz was eerily calm about his role as one of the most infamous serial killers the nation had ever seen. He even admitted to a plan to murder more innocent people at a popular nightclub in the Hamptons the night he was caught and "go down in a blaze of glory."[10]

On May 8, 1978, Berkowitz stood trial for the Son of Sam murders. He had three separate hearings with three separate justices at the Brooklyn Supreme Court to account for the crimes in Brooklyn, Queens, and the Bronx. In the hearings, which occurred consecutively, Berkowitz officially pleaded guilty to shooting 13 people and killing six. Berkowitz submitted his plea against the advice of his lawyer, Leon Stern, who insisted he plead not guilty by reason of insanity.

INSANITY PLEAS

When a person is accused of a heinous crime, he or she usually has three main plea options: not guilty, guilty, and not guilty by reason of insanity. For that person to be convicted and proven guilty, the prosecution must show not only that the accused committed a guilty act and the act was done intentionally, but also that the accused was aware of his or her actions and decisions, thinking rationally, and fully able to control his or her own behavior. In order for someone to be considered legally insane, he or she must be unable to distinguish right from wrong or understand the consequences of an action. When judging a murder case, particularly one as egregious as Berkowitz's, this can get very tricky. Many of history's most infamous serial killers have used the insanity defense in their cases, including Jeffrey Dahmer, Kenneth Bianchi, Albert Fish, and John Wayne Gacy.

A month later, on June 12, the court delivered its verdict. Berkowitz was found guilty and sentenced to prison terms of 25 years to life for each of his six murders, the maximum amount allowed at the time. Berkowitz was also sentenced to nine consecutive 25-year sentences for attempted murder, six 15-year sentences for assault, five 15-year sentences for illegal gun possession, and one seven-year sentence for weapon possession. The total added up to more than 300 years in prison.[12] Though under state law Berkowitz would be eligible for being released on parole after 25 years in prison, all three judges maintained that the likelihood of him earning parole was little to none.

"It is obviously the intention of the Court that this defendant remain incarcerated for the rest of his natural life," said Queens Supreme Court Justice Nicholas Tsoucalas.[13] Bronx Justice William Kapelman agreed. "It is not my purpose to scold you for the insidious crimes for which you have been sentenced today," he said. "Let me just say that you grovel in the depth of human degradation."[14]

Berkowitz in Prison

Following Berkowitz's sentencing, he was taken to Attica Correctional Facility, a maximum-security prison in New York. There, he was placed in a heavily guarded private cell, and he mostly kept to himself. During his first few years, he worked as a porter, pouring hot water into buckets in prisoners' cells.

In February 1979, Berkowitz held a press conference from Attica in which he shocked the world by publicly denouncing his prior claims that demons had convinced him to kill.

A RUCKUS IN THE COURTROOM

On the day of Berkowitz's trial, hundreds of people stood outside the Brooklyn courthouse, hoping to catch a glimpse of the serial killer. Some of the victims' family members got a seat inside the courtroom, eager to see justice served. One of the spectators was a friend of Stacy Moskowitz's family, 30-year-old Daniel Carrique. Carrique became so distraught by what Berkowitz had done that he rushed the podium during the trial, yelling, "You're gonna burn in hell, Berkowitz! You're gonna burn!"[15] Security guards grabbed Carrique and carried him out of the courtroom, but not before he managed to kick one of the detectives.

Berkowitz speaks at Attica prison in February 1979.

Instead, he insisted that he was getting back at a world—
and, specifically, the female gender—that had rejected him.
Around that same time, he also made similar statements to
court-appointed psychiatrist Dr. David Abrahamsen.

"Yes, it was all a hoax, a silly hoax, well planned and
thought out. . . . At the time I was committing the crimes, the
Son of Sam shootings, I felt guilty unconsciously. Therefore, I
needed to somehow justify everything in my mind," Berkowitz

"IMPULSIVE, BUT NOT INSANE"

During the Son of Sam trial, three court-appointed psychiatrists were tasked with interviewing Berkowitz to determine his mental state. Two of them came to the conclusion that he was certifiably insane. Dr. David Abrahamsen did not. He interviewed Berkowitz while Berkowitz was still in Kings County Hospital, before he was sent to prison. Abrahamsen later wrote about this experience:

> After just a single interview, it was clear to me that Berkowitz did not exhibit the symptoms of schizophrenia. And the clear-headed cunning with which he had selected the time and place of his killings and eluded for a whole year the greatest police manhunt in recent memory hardly seemed to be typical psychotic behavior. I found Berkowitz to be impulsive, but not insane; the impulses were controllable. He had a character disorder, with many hysterical traits mixed in growing from a need to call attention to himself, to make himself more important [than] he is.[17]

wrote in a letter to Abrahamsen. "This is where the 'demon' story came into being. It gave me the mental motivation and mental justification I needed at the time. However, deep down inside I knew I was the real 'demon' so to speak. It was just me, myself and I."[16]

A few months after the press conference, Berkowitz was attacked by a fellow inmate at Attica. His throat was slashed, and he almost died. Still, he continued to serve time at Attica, mostly in isolation, until 1987, when he was moved to the Sullivan Correctional Facility in upstate New York. In 2016, Berkowitz was transferred to the Shawangunk Correctional Facility in Wallkill, New York. As of 2019, he was still incarcerated there. Every time he has been up for parole since he became eligible in 2002, the parole has been denied.

CHAPTER FIVE

THE EVIDENCE

Most serial killers have been found to be conniving murderers who lack remorse for the atrocious crimes they commit. They are calculating in their approach and take great pains not to get caught. In some cases, especially those that occurred before the Integrated Automated Fingerprint Identification System (IAFIS) was established in 1999 and other technological advances boosted modern-day forensic capabilities, tracking down a serial killer was incredibly difficult.

For example, Ted Bundy kidnapped, raped, and dismembered at least 30 women from 1974 to 1978.[1] After he was caught, he escaped from jail—twice—and even killed again before being recaptured and later executed in 1989. Jeffrey Dahmer, known as the Milwaukee Cannibal, went on a killing spree for 14 years before he was captured in 1991. He murdered 17 young men before he was caught.[2] The Zodiac killer murdered at least five people in California during the

Forensic investigators use many different techniques to examine evidence.

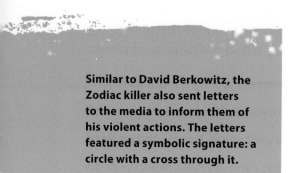

Similar to David Berkowitz, the Zodiac killer also sent letters to the media to inform them of his violent actions. The letters featured a symbolic signature: a circle with a cross through it.

1960s and 1970s. As of June 2019, police still had not figured out his identity.[3]

Given the challenges associated with investigating serial killers, how did the police finally catch Berkowitz after he had eluded them for more than a year? Similar to Ted Bundy's case, it was a parking ticket that finally did Berkowitz in. But leading up to that moment, there were many other clues and pieces of evidence that the cops were working with to try to nab the Son of Sam.

The Gun

From early on in the Son of Sam's killing spree, the NYPD looked for clues related to the gun used to shoot the victims. After Virginia Voskerichian's death on March 8, 1977, the bullets found at the crime scene linked her murder to that of Donna Lauria. It appeared that the same type of gun had been used in both killings. But just because detectives had the make and model of the gun didn't mean they could easily find its owner.

The Son of Sam had used a .44-caliber revolver, also known as the Charter Arms Bulldog, in each of his attacks. But when the cops did a systematic check to see who in New York City

A New York City police officer shows the .44-caliber revolver used by the Son of Sam at the press conference following Berkowitz's arrest.

might own such a gun, the search came up with hundreds of names. A trace on all of the .44-caliber weapons ever made came up with 28,000 registered guns.[4]

Relying on the gun to provide any major breakthroughs was described as a "needle-in-a-haystack endeavor" by Detective Dowd and other police officials working on the case.[5] The Omega task force did track down and interview everyone registered as owning a Charter Arms Bulldog in New York City. But that only covered a portion of the gun-toting

THE CHARTER ARMS BULLDOG

If Berkowitz had bought his own gun, perhaps he would have been easier to find. But the Charter Arms Bulldog had instead been purchased by Billy Dan Parker, an old army buddy of Berkowitz's. Parker bought the gun at a pawn shop called the Spring Branch Jewelry and Loan Company in Houston, Texas, on June 12, 1976—six weeks before the Son of Sam murders began. He presumably gave the gun to Berkowitz. After Berkowitz was arrested, Parker was not charged with any crime, as he had no knowledge of his friend's intent to kill. Federal agents also questioned Billy Wheeler, the man who managed the pawnshop and who sold the gun to Parker, the day after Berkowitz's arrest. Wheeler had no recollection of the gun's purchaser.

population. After all, many people, including Berkowitz, owned either unregistered guns or those that had been purchased by other people.

Unreliable Witness Testimonies

With any crime, detectives rely on eyewitness testimonies to find clues about the case. But the problem with relying on this type of evidence is that these reports are sometimes unreliable or inaccurate. Witnesses are often under a lot of pressure when questioned by the police. Sometimes, this stress influences the way they recall an event. Memories can also be faulty. Though many people claim they are certain of what they saw when a crime took place, variables sometimes interfere, including low light, noise in the area, and even the witness's ingrained racial or gender biases. In the Son of Sam case, much of the information police received was incorrect for these reasons. For example, using calls from the dedicated Son of Sam tip line, investigators put together a list of at least

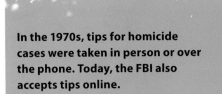

In the 1970s, tips for homicide cases were taken in person or over the phone. Today, the FBI also accepts tips online.

3,000 possible suspects. They checked every name on the list, but, perhaps unsurprisingly, the names reported to the tip line came up clean.

Because investigators weren't having much luck with the tip line, they also resorted to more unconventional methods to track down possible leads. They interviewed psychiatrists and psychologists in order to understand the killer's frame of mind. They talked to numerologists and hypnotists on the off chance that a tidbit of seemingly wacky information might hold a kernel of truth. Undercover officers even posed as young couples on lovers' lanes across Queens, Brooklyn, and the Bronx, hoping to lure the Son of Sam into their traps.

Despite these unconventional tactics, and as a result of unreliable tips and witness statements, the Omega task force took many wrong turns. After the shooting of Moskowitz and Violante on July 31, 1977, for example, eyewitness Tommy Zaino gave the police an entirely different description of the killer, as compared to the person other witnesses had described. He had

Throughout the Summer of Sam, the Omega task force tried to hone in on the make and model of the killer's getaway car. Many witnesses reported seeing a yellow Volkswagen speeding away from the crime scenes. Following up on the information, the police investigated everyone in New York with a yellow VW and cross-examined the information with the killer's description. This was yet another dead end. David Berkowitz drove a cream-colored 1970 Ford Galaxy.

"strawy hair . . . long, all out of shape, light brown hair, light blonde," Zaino said in an interview with *NBC News*.[6] For a while, the cops considered the idea that the Son of Sam was wearing a wig.

Above all, "the Son of Sam proved so elusive [because] many traditional ways of tracking down a killer had backfired," wrote *Time* magazine reporter Lily Rothman years after Berkowitz was captured. "[The] police sketches were based on unreliable witness testimony, which meant the public was on alert for someone who didn't resemble the killer. Nor was there a discernible pattern in the seemingly random murders."[7]

The Victims

When attempting to crack a case involving a serial killer, police usually look for overarching patterns to help pin down a killer's identity or style. Charles Albright, who targeted sex workers in Dallas, Texas, in 1990 and 1991, was nicknamed the "Eyeball

A dispatcher answers calls to the Son of Sam tip line in 1977. As the case commanded police officers' attention during the Summer of Sam, it also captivated the public.

Killer" because he removed his victims' eyes after murdering them. Canadian American Keith Jesperson, a truck driver who murdered at least eight women in the United States during the early 1990s, was called the "Happy Face Killer" because he left hand-drawn smiley faces at some of his crime scenes and on his letters to the media at the time of the attacks.[8]

In Berkowitz's case, his victims had similar characteristics. All of them were young and had just come from a dance club

SERIAL KILLERS' MOTIVES

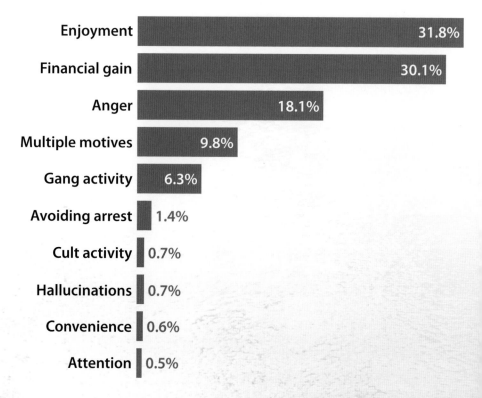

Motive	Percentage
Enjoyment	31.8%
Financial gain	30.1%
Anger	18.1%
Multiple motives	9.8%
Gang activity	6.3%
Avoiding arrest	1.4%
Cult activity	0.7%
Hallucinations	0.7%
Convenience	0.6%
Attention	0.5%

Investigators in the Son of Sam case were never able to pin down Berkowitz's exact motive for the killings, though they had many theories. Dr. Mike Aamodt of Radford University conducted a study on serial killers. Some of the results are shown above. Aamodt concluded that most serial killers have addictive personalities and get pleasure from the power and control they have over their victims.[9]

or movie. Most of them had long brown or black hair. There was enough of a physical resemblance between everyone he attacked that long-haired women and men across New York City started taking precautions to protect themselves. They cut or dyed their hair. Wig sales across the city spiked. "The girls were scared out of their living daylights. When he was doing his thing, people didn't want to go to clubs because people felt that they were the next target," said Detective Justus. "He was out there, girls were dying, and they were cautious and went out in groups and changed their hair color."[10]

Stacy Moskowitz's murder heightened this fear among New Yorkers. Unlike every other Son of Sam victim, Moskowitz was killed in Brooklyn, not in the Bronx or Queens. Instead of a brunette, Moskowitz was blonde. The change in the Son of Sam's pattern sent a shock wave through the city. "Even I felt safe until now. After the two were shot in Bayside, we were bombarded with brown-haired women who wanted haircuts. Now I am waiting for blondes to call . . . you don't have to have long dark hair to be shot," hairdresser Mary Ann Boroz told the *New York Times* at the time.[11] A customer at Hair Touch barber shop offered a similar opinion. "This one really did it," the customer said. "Girls are staying home and you know it could be anyone. It's the pattern that has been changed. You just don't know what he's going to do next."[12]

As New Yorkers worried about the Son of Sam, a cab driver displayed an NYPD poster with information about the killer.

Whether in the Bronx, Brooklyn, or Queens, using a knife (as in his first attack on Christmas Eve, 1975) or the Charter Arms Bulldog revolver, it was clear that Berkowitz was determined to kill. His actions incited fear in the hearts and minds of people

across the nation. But it was the press—and the letters that

Berkowitz sent to *Daily News* reporter Jimmy Breslin—that

stoked the flames.

CHAPTER SIX

A MEDIA FRENZY

On May 30, 1977, reporter Jimmy Breslin walked into his office at the *Daily News* to discover something chilling—a letter from the legendary Son of Sam. It was addressed directly to Breslin. The letter read:

> J.B., I'm just dropping you a line to let you know that I appreciate your interest in those recent and horrendous .44 killings. I also want to tell you that I read your column daily and find it quite informative. Tell me, Jim, what will you have for July Twenty-Ninth? You can forget about me if you like because I don't care for publicity. However, you must not forget Donna Lauria and you cannot let the people forget her, either. She was a very sweet girl but Sam's a thirsty lad and he won't let me stop killing until he gets his fill of blood.[1]

For the next 24 hours, Breslin consulted with the police about what to do with the note. They analyzed it for

New York Daily News **journalist Jimmy Breslin,** *left*, **was known for his work reporting on the Son of Sam killings.**

COPYCAT KILLING?

When Jimmy Breslin received the letter from the Son of Sam, he immediately told the police about it. Breslin and his staff also compared the note to the first one left at the April 17, 1977, crime scene of Alexander Esau and Valentina Suriani's murders. The letter to Breslin was longer than the one addressed to Captain Joseph Borrelli. It also was written in a more sophisticated manner than the first letter. This led detectives working on the case to suspect that the Breslin letter was either a fake or that the murder had been perpetrated by a copycat killer. Copycat killings are murders committed by someone other than the original killer, hoping to receive similar fame. As history has revealed, both of these theories were incorrect. The letter to Breslin turned out to be written by Berkowitz.

fingerprints. They read each paragraph dozens of times to uncover possible clues. Finally, in an attempt to entice the killer to go public, they decided to run it in the newspaper.

On June 5, the people of New York woke up to find an alarming headline splashed across the front page of the *Daily News*: "Breslin to .44 Killer: Give Up! It's Only Way Out."[2] Inside the article was an even bigger surprise: the complete text of the Son of Sam's letter to Breslin.

The foreboding correspondence was the first of many that Breslin would receive from Berkowitz, both before and after the serial killer's capture. But instead of considering it a warning, Breslin and his colleagues used the letter as a tool in their work, aiming to sell more papers than any of their competitors. In doing so, the *Daily News* helped pull the public into a terrified panic. "The frenzied coverage fanned the growing sense of fear;

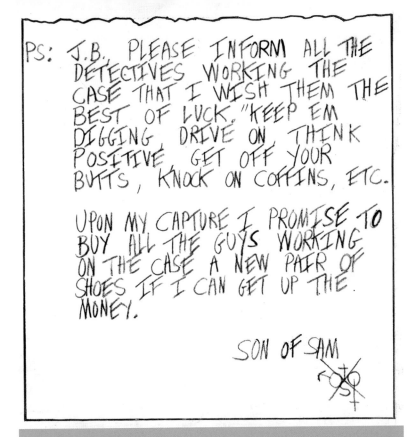

PS: J.B. PLEASE INFORM ALL THE DETECTIVES WORKING THE CASE THAT I WISH THEM THE BEST OF LUCK. "KEEP EM DIGGING, DRIVE ON, THINK POSITIVE, GET OFF YOUR BUTTS, KNOCK ON COFFINS, ETC.

UPON MY CAPTURE I PROMISE TO BUY ALL THE GUYS WORKING ON THE CASE A NEW PAIR OF SHOES IF I CAN GET UP THE MONEY.

SON OF SAM

Part of the letter written to reporter Jimmy Breslin from the Son of Sam

the growing sense of fear fanned the frenzied coverage," wrote Jonathan Mahler in his book *Ladies and Gentlemen, The Bronx Is Burning*, which focuses on 1977 in New York City.[3]

"A Tabloid Perfect Storm"

In professional journalism, there are many different ways to write a news story. The traditional approach is based on impartial, objective reporting and getting facts across. These types of articles discuss what happened, where and how it happened, and who was involved. For example, today, mainstream newspapers such as the *New York Times* and the

Washington Post focus on this type of reporting. In contrast, tabloid journalism emphasizes sensationalism. These types of stories often highlight salacious details about crimes committed, rely on celebrity gossip, or include outlandish accounts that may stretch the truth. During the Summer of Sam, the *Daily News* was the epitome of tabloid-style journalism, and people couldn't get enough of the paper's captivating coverage.

But the *Daily News* wasn't the only paper trying to get a lead on what was turning out to be one of the biggest news stories of the decade. Throughout 1976 and 1977, the *New York Times*, the *New Yorker* magazine, and other publications followed suit, publishing daily articles on anything they could find about the

JIMMY BRESLIN'S REPORTING

Throughout Jimmy Breslin's coverage of the Son of Sam serial murders, he was known for producing columns that read almost like drama-heavy fictional stories. For the newspaper's readers, the effect was riveting. But when compared with today's standards at many newspapers, the language and tone of Breslin's articles were far from objective.

For example, on the day the *Daily News* ran the Son of Sam's correspondence, the newspaper also printed Breslin's play-by-play of the hours he spent in Donna Lauria's parents' apartment after they agreed to be interviewed. At one point, Breslin wrote, "The only way for the killer to leave this special torment is to give himself up to me, if he trusts me, to the police, and receive both help and safety. If he wants any further contact, all he has to do is call or write me at the *Daily News*. It's simple to get me. The only people I don't answer are bill collectors."[4]

Son of Sam murders or the mysterious identity of the killer. But no paper was more of a rival to the *Daily News* at the time than the *New York Post*. The two newspapers were locked in a fight for subscribers, and the Son of Sam killings were the perfect tabloid story that could keep readers hooked. "It had absolutely everything going for it as a tabloid perfect storm," said Sam Roberts, a *New York Times* reporter who was the *Daily News* city editor in 1977. "It was an ongoing, unfolding crime story that New Yorkers were genuinely terrified about."[5]

For example, before the *Daily News* printed its article containing the Son of Sam's letter to Breslin, the paper ran days of teasers that speculated on what the contents of the letter might be. In response, the editors at the *New York Post* directed

A DEADLY INFLUENCE

When thinking about what compels serial killers to commit murder multiple times, it can be difficult to point to the motivating factors. Ronald M. Holmes, a retired criminal justice professor, has worked on more than 500 criminal profiles for various police departments. He suggests all the back-and-forth between the newspapers might have prompted Berkowitz to continue his killing spree. "I believe that the press does 'help' in the commission of some crimes, especially serial murder," Holmes explained to *Rolling Stone*. "[Serial killers] have a sense of invincibility, and their fantasies are so strong that the news about their crimes only goes on to convince them that [they] cannot be caught and 'must' continue on with their predations."[6]

Police officers read the *Daily News* the day after Berkowitz was arrested.

their star reporter, Steve Dunleavy, to write stories containing even the smallest details surrounding the case. Sometimes, that meant reporting on anonymous tips, even if the clues were obviously inconsequential. In his reporting for one article, Dunleavy spent 13 hours at the hospital with Stacy Moskowitz's and Robert Violante's parents as Moskowitz lay dying, in order to get a scoop on the *Daily News*. Dunleavy wrote:

For 13 1/2 hours a Post *reporter stood at the side of four courageous people in a painful and often stirring vigil—praying, talking about God and swearing at an unknown madman who has launched a guerrilla war against the young and beautiful of this city. This vigil bound together Jerry and Neysa Moskowitz, who are Jewish, with Pat and Teresa Violante, an Italian Catholic family. Never before has this reporter seen such pain, strength and old-fashioned guts.*[7]

The media frenzy around the Son of Sam continued even after Berkowitz was captured. The day after Berkowitz's arrest, the *Post* ran another front-page story about Berkowitz headlined "Caught!"[8] But the headline had an unintended connection. Four reporters, one each from the *Post*, the *Daily News*, *Time* magazine, and the *Washington Post*, had actually tried to sneak into Berkowitz's Yonkers apartment to get a scoop on the story. They were arrested. Still, both the *Post* and the *Daily News* sold millions of copies the day after Berkowitz was caught—far more than the amount sold on a regular news day.

In another attempt to one-up Breslin, Dunleavy crafted an article with the

In objective news stories, it is a reporter's job to separate fact from fiction and write the truth. Information is gathered by reporters and fact-checked by editors. Then it is turned into an article for a newspaper or magazine or aired on TV or the radio.

headline, "How I Became a Mass Killer."[9] It showed excerpts from a series of letters supposedly written from the accused Son of Sam to his childhood love interest. The article ran on the front page of the *New York Post* and featured David Berkowitz's name as the byline. It was a tactic no one had seen before—and it had an immediate explosive effect.

"Son of Sam established Steve as a force to be reckoned with, and it shot the *Post*'s circulation way [up]," *Rolling Stone* reporter Chet Flippo wrote years later. "[The] *News* and the *Post* fought daily over Sam. . . . This was high-quality crime, worthy of New York tabloid journalism. . . . Dunleavy and Breslin were locked in a bitter struggle. Which one could produce the day's best Son of Sam story?"[10]

Far-Reaching Effects

For many reasons, the battle between the *Daily News* and the *New York Post* had far-reaching effects on the way the media continued to report the news—and how the public received it. Before the Son of Sam phenomenon, most local crimes were included in the local news sections of smaller newspapers. The style of journalism was more restrained, and stories didn't really spread to the front page at major newspapers and magazines or TV broadcasting nationwide.

But after the Berkowitz case, Breslin and Dunleavy's aggressive, sensationalistic style became more common at other papers in New York and major cities across the United States. "I think the Son of Sam murders really kind of broke new ground for sensationalism by the tabloid press of New York," said Mark Feldstein, a media historian and professor at the University of Maryland's Philip Merrill College of Journalism.[12]

In other words, a reporter's job became not just about stating facts; it was also crucial to attract as many new subscribers as possible. According to *Rolling Stone*'s Cady Drell, the approach is still relevant today. While there's not exactly

BERKOWITZ'S TAKE ON THE MEDIA

In 2013, psychologist Scott Bonn interviewed Berkowitz while he was in prison. Bonn was doing research for a book called *Why We Love Serial Killers: The Curious Appeal of the World's Most Savage Murderers*. Over two years, Bonn asked Berkowitz hundreds of questions, including his thoughts about why the public—and the media—are so fascinated by serial murderers. Berkowitz told Bonn:

> Concerning 'evil,' perhaps everyone has the potential, under the right conditions and circumstances, to do terrible, horrendous things. . . . People want to understand why. The media take a part in this, too, especially with serial crimes. Serial killers are very rare. All of the media attention makes them look more prevalent than they really are. In my opinion, this is part of the inner spiritual decline of western society as we slowly slide towards anarchy.[13]

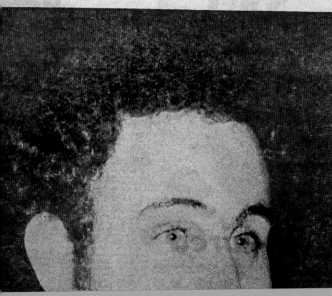

NEW YORK POST

THURSDAY, AUGUST 11, 1977 25 CENTS   Vol. 176, No. 225   © 1977 The New York Post Corporation

METRO
TODAY'S RACING

DAILY PAID CIRCULATION 2D QUARTER 1977   609,39

AY
Cloudy, 85-90
GHT
Cloudy, low 70s
ORROW
90s
page 2
*AGE 34

CAUGHT!

Son of Sam was on way to kill again

'I wanted to go out in a blaze of glory'

By CARL J. PELLECK

The man police say is the Son of Sam was on his way to claim more victims whe he walked into the arms of waiting detec tives.

David Berkowitz, 24, had already writ ten a letter—his third—addressed to Suf folk County and New York police and the press. He was going to leave it alongside his latest victim. It had no stamp on it.

In questioning after his arrest last night, Ber kowitz said he hadn't quite made up his mind

Media experts say the Son of Sam rivalry between the *New York Daily News* and the *New York Post* has had lasting effects on the media industry.

a direct correlation between the Son of Sam coverage to the online clickbait of the modern era, the similarities are obvious. Drell wrote:

> Stories only mildly relevant to the actual news getting
>
> above-the-fold attention, hot takes that are less fact and more
>
> fact-adjacent sucking all the air out of the room, shaping the

74

★ ★ ★
FINAL

Vol. 59. No. 41

DAILY ◎ NEWS

Partly cloudy today.
Upper 80s. Cloudy,
showers tomorrow.
Details page 63.

New York, Friday, August 12, 1977

Price: 20 cents

SAM CHANGED AFTER LSD TRIPS

Took Drugs as Soldier in Korea

Exclusive

Hero Witness'
Own Story

Page 2

way the public takes in any given story. Cable and Internet news, wildly reliant on this approach, seem like direct descendants of the new media norm that the competing dailies created around the Son of Sam. With their handling of the case, the tabloids showed that they could pad out a salacious story by harping on the parts most likely to shock and terrify—and the rest of the media hasn't looked back.[14]

75

CHAPTER SEVEN

CONSPIRACY THEORIES

I n some cases, regardless of media reporting or police investigation, it is still difficult to determine what actually happened—or at least some people think it is. This is when conspiracy theories are born. In simplest terms, a conspiracy theory is just an alternate explanation for something that happened. Conspiracy theories are beliefs that reject the standard explanation for an event and instead credit a covert group or organization with carrying out a secret plot that is largely unknown or unrecognized by the general public.

After Berkowitz's arrest on August 10, 1977, the NYPD publicly announced it had captured the Son of Sam. In a statement to the press, police officials said Berkowitz said he was the sole gunman, responsible for all eight shootings. It was a clear conclusion to the case.

In the years since Berkowitz was arrested and convicted, people have developed theories about whether he was the only assailant in the Son of Sam killings.

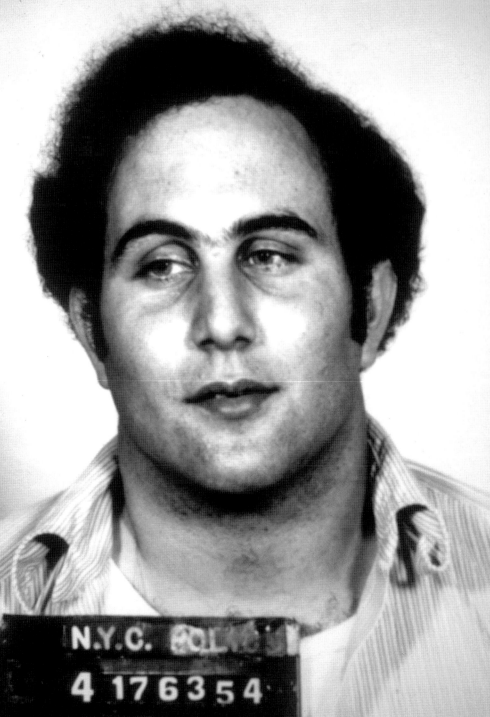

But some people weren't so sure. Even after Berkowitz was physically behind bars, multiple theories about who had really committed the Son of Sam killings persisted. Conspiracy theorists insisted there was much more to the story. In particular, they wondered whether there was more than one killer.

A Collaborative Effort

It's true that after Berkowitz was arrested, he admitted to shooting his victims without being coerced. But in statements from prison years later, when he had nothing else to lose, he said he didn't act alone. What's more, some people believed him, including the police in Yonkers and the district attorney in Queens, where five of the shootings took place. "I believe David Berkowitz did not act alone, that in fact others did cooperate, aid and abet him in the commission of these crimes," District

Attorney John Santucci said in 1979. "In fact, it has crossed my mind that this 44-caliber pistol was passed around among a number of people."[1]

In the 1990s, Berkowitz did a prison interview with author Maury Terry, who was writing a book about the case. Berkowitz told Terry he was part of a group of people from Yonkers called Process Church of the Final Judgment that were involved in satanic rituals. He said they participated in animal sacrifices and child pornography, meeting often in the woodsy grounds of Yonkers's Untermyer Park.

Berkowitz divulged that some members of the group had also planned a set of murders as a sort of offering to Satan. Yes, Berkowitz told Terry, he had played a major role in these murders, but he wasn't always the shooter. In fact, according to Berkowitz's own admission, he was the gunman at only two of the eight shootings attributed to the Son of Sam. He said

A CONNECTION TO JIMI HENDRIX

The Omega task force used a lot of unconventional tactics to try to solve the Son of Sam's murders, including considering some far-fetched theories. One particularly wacky conspiracy theory was that Berkowitz had gotten his nickname from a 1967 Jimi Hendrix Experience record. An anonymous person called the Son of Sam tip line to suggest the idea. Apparently, one song, "Purple Haze," can be heard with a faint chanting, "Help me, help me, help me, son of Sam, son of Sam." Though some Operation Omega detectives entertained the idea, Captain Joseph Borrelli wasn't convinced. "It's interesting. It could be a coincidence," he said. "At this particular moment, I don't think it deserves special attention."[2]

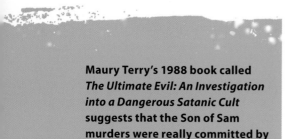

Maury Terry's 1988 book called *The Ultimate Evil: An Investigation into a Dangerous Satanic Cult* suggests that the Son of Sam murders were really committed by a group of devil worshippers who were never caught.

that he had killed three of the six victims, only those murdered in the Bronx.

"The killings were another sacrifice to our gods, bunch of scumbags that they were. . . . We made a pact, maybe with the devil, but also with each other. . . . We were going to go all the way with this thing. We're soldiers of Satan now. I was just too far in, too loyal, too much playing the role of the soldier and trying to please people," Berkowitz said.[3] He added that he was present for all of the killings. "[I was] in the area, and scouting, and I had a part. I'm responsible for my involvement in those things, and, you know, definitely guilty," he said.[4]

In that interview, Berkowitz then named some of his alleged accomplices for the first time, including John and Michael Carr, Sam Carr's sons. He mapped out the shooter's escape route during the Stacy Moskowitz murder and revealed that the shooter—not him—was the one apparently driving a yellow Volkswagen. This would explain why many eyewitnesses claim they saw a yellow car fleeing the scene, not Berkowitz's cream-colored Ford Galaxy.

Berkowitz photographed in jail in 1995

According to *New York* magazine, the police sketches from the other shootings where Berkowitz claimed John Carr had pulled the trigger don't actually resemble Berkowitz. They look like someone else.

Neither John nor Michael Carr were alive at the time to verify or disprove Berkowitz's story. John Carr died at a motel in North Dakota in 1978, reportedly from a self-inflicted gunshot wound. Michael Carr was in a one-car drunken driving accident on the West Side Highway a year later and didn't survive his injuries. The strange part about Michael Carr's death was that he apparently had a clinical distaste for alcohol and didn't drink. Some conspiracy theorists believe the Carr brothers' deaths weren't suicides or accidents, but criminal homicides. The theory states they were murdered to cover up their role in the Son of Sam's killing spree.

Case Reopened

By the time Berkowitz was captured and the killings stopped, the public was anxious to move on from the issue. People were eager to free themselves from the fear that had taunted them for more than a year. Though some of the cops or attorneys working on the case, such as Santucci, weren't totally convinced they had all the facts straight, they were more than ready to move on to other pressing cases—except for Yonkers police Sergeant Mike Novotny.

In 1996, Novotny and the rest of the Yonkers Police Department reopened the Son of Sam case to investigate the multiple-gunmen theory. In an interview with reporter John Hockenberry, Novotny hinted that at least "half a dozen" people could've been involved in the murders.[5] Though they haven't yet found any definite links or new evidence to suggest it's more than just a conspiracy theory, the case remains suspended—but not yet closed—as of 2019, for the foreseeable future. This means the case is not actively being investigated, but it is not considered solved either.

This brings a little comfort to some of the victims who are still alive, many of whom are still unsure of what to believe. Carl Denaro, who was shot in October 1976 in Queens, claims

RUMORS VERIFIED?

There have been numerous attempts over the years to verify whether Berkowitz's multiple-shooter claims are true. Detective James Rothstein worked for the NYPD in Manhattan at the time of the Son of Sam murders. In a 2004 interview, he recalled some of the leads he had followed at least five years before Berkowitz even arrived on the scene. They involved a Yonkers-based cult involved in pedophilia, similar to the one Berkowitz mentioned years later during his prison interview with Maury Terry.

"We got information that children were being used and in particular there was something strange going on in Van Courtland Park and Untermyer Park," Rothstein said. He added that there was evidence of animal sacrifice. "It came down that somebody was murdering German shepherds," he said.[6] Rothstein also remembered seeing a building in the park covered in satanic symbols—the same symbols found on Berkowitz's apartment walls after he was arrested.

Despite conspiracy theories about the Son of Sam, the NYPD maintains its
conclusion that Berkowitz was the killer.

Berkowitz couldn't have killed that many people without help. "There's no way that David Berkowitz did all the shootings. I personally think it was a cult," he told *NBC News*. "I don't know that for a fact. But I am convinced that—and no one can unconvince me—that more than one person was involved."[7]

Psychologist Scott Bonn disagrees. In a 2017 interview for *Deadline*, Bonn maintained that Berkowitz was addicted to killing and had pulled off the murder spree on his own. "For Berkowitz, as a serial killer, he loved to kill and needed to kill," Bonn said. "Why he did it can be traced back to a childhood fear when he was abandoned by his birth mother and adopted as a child. He grew up to be a frightened and angry, raging individual. He was striking back at society and did it in a way that held the entire city of New York hostage for a year."[8]

As for NYPD homicide Detective Bill Clark, he maintains that the department's handling of the case and the conviction of Berkowitz as the sole gunman was solid. "For [Berkowitz] to say years later that he was part of a cult, you know, it's just more attention," Clark said. "That's all it's about with him."[9]

CHAPTER EIGHT

BERKOWITZ'S LEGACY

It has been more than 40 years since the Son of Sam stalked the streets of New York City. Yet he is still one of the country's most notorious serial killers. Since his arrest in 1977, Berkowitz has bounced around between maximum-security correctional facilities, from Attica to Sullivan to Shawangunk. It is likely he will spend the rest of his life in prison.

Looking back on the Summer of Sam, some of Berkowitz's targets who are alive are still bitter about the attacks. Robert Violante never got married or had any children after the shooting. He spent years trying to get over the stress of what had happened and had hoped for Berkowitz to be sentenced to the death penalty, even though that was not legally an option at the time. "He ruined not just my life, 12 other lives, plus their families," Violante told *CBS News*. "So, how do you forgive something like that, somebody like that? You don't."[1]

The Son of Sam case remains well known and has continued to be examined by the media and others, such as this panel related to a TV special in 2017.

THE DEATH PENALTY IN NEW YORK

Capital punishment has a bumpy history in New York. The state had the second-highest number of executions of any state from 1608 to 1972, after Virginia. In 1890, William Kemmler, who murdered his wife with a hatchet, became the first person to be executed in an electric chair.

In the 1970s, everything changed. In 1972, the US Supreme Court invalidated all death penalty statutes in the country. A year later, the New York state legislature called for a mandatory death sentence for the murder of a police officer or correctional officer or a murder committed in prison by an inmate serving a life sentence. But in 1977 and 1984, those terms were eliminated, and the death penalty was abolished in the state, which was why it could not be applied to Berkowitz's case. Though capital punishment was reinstated in 1995, it was declared unconstitutional by the New York Court of Appeals in 2004. As of 2008, execution equipment has been removed from the state's correctional facilities.

Though Jody Valenti eventually worked through much of her trauma from the shooting, she still struggles with seeing the fame and attention Berkowitz continues to receive in the press, especially during anniversaries of the murders. "What are we celebrating? The lunatic that's in prison for life who's getting benefits?" she asked. "He's getting three square meals. He's getting an education. He's getting everything he needs, and I find it very disturbing."[2]

Donna DeMasi, too, has grappled with mixed feelings over the years. But she is glad Berkowitz is still behind bars. "I feel people can change—let him change in jail," she told InsideEdition.com. "He is never going to come out. I will never see him and never have to see him and I am thankful."[3]

As for Berkowitz, he refutes the idea that he's the same brutal murderer he once was. In fact, he says he feels remorseful for all the pain he caused the victims and their families. "Unfortunately, it was a terrible tragedy. I regret that with all my heart," Berkowitz told the *New York Post* in 2016. "It was a time that my life was out of control. I'd do anything if I could go back and change that, but it's impossible to go back into the past and fix those kinds of things."[4]

LIFE IN A MAXIMUM-SECURITY PRISON

Shawangunk Correctional Facility, located in Wallkill, New York, opened in 1983. It can hold 558 inmates.[5] The prison offers psychiatric counseling and treatment for alcohol and substance abuse. If an inmate is incarcerated for a sex crime, he is required to participate in a counseling and treatment program specific to sex offenders. But life in a maximum-security prison isn't like what one might see on television. It's fairly brutal, often full of violent outbursts, gang rivalries, and mandatory periods of prolonged isolation for the most serious criminals.

Fame, Not Fortune

Since Berkowitz was sent to prison, he has had ample time to reflect on his crimes. He's also been offered many opportunities to tell his story. The interviews he conducted with Bonn, Abrahamsen, and others provided volumes of material for high-profile books, including Bonn's *Why We Love Serial Killers:*

The Curious Appeal of the World's Most Savage Murderers and Lawrence Klausner's *Son of Sam: Based on the Authorized Transcription of the Tapes, Official Documents and Diaries of David Berkowitz.* There have also been several documentaries about the case, such as the Smithsonian Channel's 2017 documentary *The Lost Tapes: Son of Sam*, the 2017 made-for-TV movie *Son of Sam: The Hunt for a Killer*, and perhaps most famously, Spike Lee's 1999 film, *Summer of Sam*, which focused on the residents of an Italian American northeast Bronx neighborhood.

REPORTER TURNED AUTHOR

At the height of the Son of Sam murders, *Daily News* columnist Jimmy Breslin was working around the clock, six days a week. He became so obsessed with his work that he moved his family out of Forest Hills, Queens, for fear of retribution from the killer. He also started working on a novel about the crimes with the director of WNBC-TV Sports, Dick Schaap. In 1978, a publisher gave Breslin $350,000 in advance for the novel and promised to print 50,000 copies of the book once it was completed. It took Breslin and Schaap seven months to write *.44*, which was published later that year. However, the book's sales weren't as high as expected, and some critics, such as a reporter from the *New York Times*, said the book was exploitive. Breslin wasn't fazed by the public's rejection. "Critics are jealous," he said in an interview. "I was part of the story. I did the book for the money. What did everyone expect me to do?"[7]

But though he is the subject of such fascination and research, Berkowitz doesn't have access to the internet in jail. He also isn't allowed to receive any money from these projects because of the horrific nature of his crimes. In 1977, New York became the first state to pass a law that prevented a convicted criminal from receiving money by selling his or her story rights to a publisher or movie producer after Berkowitz tried to sell his exclusive story rights. Since that time, 42 states and the federal government have set up similar statutes. They are called the Son of Sam laws.[8] Though the US Supreme Court deemed many of these laws unconstitutional in 1991 due to free-speech restrictions, most states chose to amend the laws to fit the court's guidelines and maintain the restriction on media profits for convicted criminals, rather than do away with the laws altogether.

Son of Hope

Because of the Son of Sam laws, Berkowitz is restricted from publishing content with a major publishing house or receiving any profit from endeavors related to the Son of Sam. But ever since his conversion to Christianity in 1987, Berkowitz has spent most of his energy working on faith-based projects dedicated to health, healing, and repentance. In 2006, he published a book of his journals entitled *Son of Hope: The Prison Journals of David Berkowitz*, despite being unable to profit from the

Decades after the Son of Sam killings, Berkowitz, shown here in 2017, says he has become a dedicated Christian and preaches from prison.

book. Berkowitz became
a minister to likeminded
inminded inmates, who call him

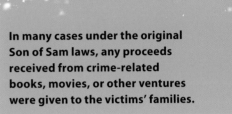

In many cases under the original Son of Sam laws, any proceeds received from crime-related books, movies, or other ventures were given to the victims' families.

"Brother Dave." "For
many years I have worked
as . . . just like a caregiver,"
he told online magazine
Salon in 2016. "I have a heart for helping and reaching out to
inmates, offenders who have psychiatric problems, who have
a lot of depression, and things like that . . . so, I feel that's my
calling in life."[9]

Over the years, Berkowitz has also worked to educate young
people. He participates in school-based projects for students
in criminology and psychology who are interested in learning
more about the criminal justice system and the psychology
behind committing crimes. "One of his goals is to warn young
people on the road to destruction," says minister Roxanne
Tauriello, who regularly visits Berkowitz in prison. "One of his
ministries is to reach out to young people to show them the
consequences of [their] actions."[10]

For those close to the Son of Sam story, Berkowitz's
transformation from serial killer to healer seems unfathomable.
The road to his supposed rebirth was somewhat of a fluke.
In 1997, he participated in an interview with televangelist Pat
Robertson's *700 Club*, a program that appears on the Christian

Broadcasting Network. Robertson praised Berkowitz's efforts to renounce the devil and redeem himself in the eyes of God.

Congregations of evangelical Christian churches noticed Berkowitz's interview with Robertson. One group in San Diego, California, called House Upon the Rock, created "The Official Home Page of David Berkowitz," which later became ForgivenForLife.com.[11] A few years later, another group of followers created AriseAndShine.org. This website hosts Berkowitz's journals and essays from 2005 to the present, written and video interviews with Berkowitz, photographs of him smiling, his official apology to his victims, and several other resources, including ministry tools and advice to parents and teens.

A VISITOR FROM THE PAST

Thirty-year-old Shayna Glassman is fully aware that her father, Craig Glassman, would not have wanted her to have contact with the Son of Sam serial killer. But now that Craig Glassman, who was Berkowitz's former downstairs neighbor, is dead, he no longer has a say over his daughter's decisions. In 2017, Shayna Glassman told *CBS News* that visiting Berkowitz in prison was weirdly fascinating. "There was something deeper I needed to get," she said. "It's my way of being with my father. The one thing he left me was this story." Since visiting Berkowitz for the first time in December 2016, Glassman has visited him at least three more times. She also bought a manual typewriter in order to write him letters. "I'm not sure what word to use to describe our relationship," she said. "There's no romance, but it's romantic because I was doing book reports about him since eighth grade. He was always part of my consciousness."[12]

In response to Berkowitz's near-constant preaching and messages of good faith, people all over the world have mailed him letters in prison. He has received thousands thus far. "Hey Berkoman!" one correspondent wrote. "I don't care what you've done in your past. I think of you as a dad. . . . You are like the best role model ever! . . . When I pray for you, I feel loved. . . . I want a life like you are living today."[13]

Failing Health

Aside from Berkowitz's shift in attitude, not much has changed for the supposedly reformed serial killer while he has been in prison. But his health has suffered a setback. On December 12, 2017, Berkowitz was transferred to a nearby hospital from prison. He had had a heart attack and needed immediate surgery. Then, on January 21, 2018, he was back in the hospital due to complications. Five days later, he was sent back to Shawangunk to recover. As of 2019, the 65-year-old remained in prison and spent much of his time preaching.

The chances of Berkowitz getting out on parole are still slim. For a man who has spent most of his adult years in prison, life on the outside would undoubtedly be different and difficult. His father, Nathan Berkowitz, died in 2012, and he's still estranged from his half-sister and stepsister. Sometimes, Berkowitz admits to thinking about what life would have been

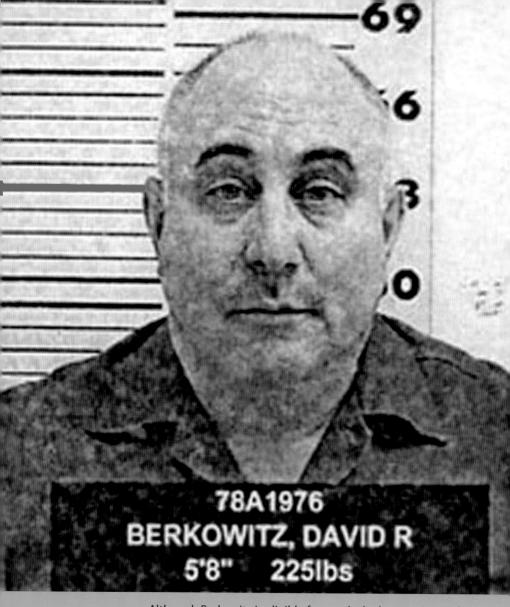

Although Berkowitz is eligible for parole, he has continuously been denied release. Experts believe he will likely remain in prison for the rest of his life.

like if he hadn't become the Son of Sam and "didn't take those wrong turns."[14]

"I have regrets about all the people I hurt, about what my life would have been like. I've missed out on a lot. But God has

given me peace about my situation," he told the *Daily News* in 2012. "I'll be the first to say that I don't deserve to have my life spared, but I believe God spared my life for me to do the things I'm doing now."[15]

TIMELINE

1953

- On June 1, David Berkowitz is born in Brooklyn, New York.

1971

- Berkowitz joins the US Army and serves for three years, one of which is spent in South Korea.

1974

- Berkowitz returns to New York and moves into various apartments before finally settling in Yonkers, a suburb of New York City. He grows increasingly disturbed by his neighbor, Sam Carr, and claims he's being possessed by Carr's dog, Harvey.

1975

- On December 24, Berkowitz stabs Michelle Forman and an unidentified woman, committing his first violent crime.

1976

- On July 29, Berkowitz fatally shoots Donna Lauria and wounds Jody Valenti in the Bronx.

- On October 23, Berkowitz shoots at Carl Denaro and Rosemary Keenan in Queens. Both survive.

- On November 27, Berkowitz shoots Donna DeMasi and Joanne Lomino in Queens. Both survive, though Lomino is injured.

1977

- On January 30, Berkowitz shoots at John Diel and his fiancée, Christine Freund, in Queens. Freund dies.

- On March 8, Berkowitz fatally shoots Virginia Voskerichian, a Columbia University student, in Queens. The NYPD is able to link this crime to previous shootings after a bullet is found on the scene.

- On April 17, Berkowitz murders Alexander Esau and Valentina Suriani in the Bronx. He leaves his first letter, signed "Son of Sam."

- On May 30, *Daily News* columnist Jimmy Breslin receives a handwritten letter from Berkowitz. Breslin later calls on the killer to surrender.

- On June 26, Berkowitz shoots Sal Lupo and Judy Placido in Queens. Both survive.

- On July 31, Berkowitz strikes again, killing Stacy Moskowitz and wounding Robert Violante. This is the Son of Sam's first crime in Brooklyn.

- On August 10, Berkowitz is arrested in connection with the Son of Sam killings.

- On August 11, Berkowitz confesses to killing six people and wounding seven. He admits he is the Son of Sam.

1978

- On May 8, Berkowitz pleads guilty to shooting at 13 people and killing six.

- On June 12, Berkowitz is given six consecutive 25-years-to-life sentences for the murders, among other charges.

1979

- On July 10, Berkowitz is stabbed in his neck in prison and nearly dies.

1987

- Berkowitz is transferred to Sullivan Correctional Facility in upstate New York.

2016

- Berkowitz is transferred to Shawangunk Correctional Facility in Wallkill, New York.

2019

- Berkowitz is consistently denied parole and remains incarcerated for his crimes.

ESSENTIAL FACTS

SIGNIFICANT EVENTS

- On June 1, 1953, Richard David Falco is born in Brooklyn, New York. He is given up by his birth mother and adopted by Nathan and Pearl Berkowitz, who change his name to David Richard Berkowitz.

- On July 29, 1976, Berkowitz begins his killing spree by shooting Donna Lauria and Jody Valenti with a .44-caliber handgun in the Bronx. Valenti survives, but Lauria does not.

- On August 10, 1977, the Son of Sam killing spree comes to an end. Acting on a tip from Cacilia Davis, the NYPD searches Berkowitz's car at his Yonkers apartment building and finds the .44-caliber gun, a rifle, ammunition, maps of the crime scenes, and another Son of Sam letter to the NYPD. The cops arrest Berkowitz as he leaves his apartment.

- On June 12, 1978, Berkowitz is given six consecutive 25-years-to-life sentences, among other charges. He is first sent to Attica Correctional Facility, a maximum-security prison in Attica, New York, then later transferred to other maximum-security prisons.

- In 1987, Berkowitz converts to Christianity. He claims he is repenting for his crimes and wants to help others heal.

KEY PLAYERS

- David Berkowitz, also known as the Son of Sam, was one of the most notorious serial killers in United States history. He murdered six people and wounded seven.

- Captain Joseph Borrelli was the head of the Queens NYPD homicide unit at the time of the Son of Sam killings.

- Jimmy Breslin was a columnist for the *Daily News* during the Son of Sam murders. He and *New York Post* reporter Steve Dunleavy competed to see who could write the most headline-grabbing coverage of the case.

- Donna Lauria was the first victim killed by the Son of Sam. She was 18 when she was murdered in the Bronx.

- Stacy Moskowitz was the last victim killed by the Son of Sam. A crucial clue at the scene of her murder—a parking ticket—led to Berkowitz's capture.

IMPACT ON SOCIETY

David Berkowitz, also known as the Son of Sam, is one of the most famous serial killers in the United States. For a little less than 12 months, he haunted the darkened streets of the Bronx, Queens, and Brooklyn in New York City, searching for mostly young women with long brown hair to kill. By the time his killing spree was over in August 1977, he had murdered six people and injured seven others. But Berkowitz's influence stretched far beyond the lives of his victims and their families. During what is commonly referred to as the Summer of Sam, people throughout the city were afraid to go out or be alone on the street. Berkowitz's ruthless acts sparked a vicious media war between the New York tabloids, especially the *New York Post* and the *New York Daily News*. After he was captured, his efforts to try to get compensated for interviews sparked the first iteration of the Son of Sam laws, statutes that prevented violent criminals from profiting from books, movies, television shows, and other types of media coverage related to their crimes.

QUOTE

"The girls were scared out of their living daylights. When [Son of Sam] was doing his thing, people didn't want to go to clubs because people felt that they were the next target. He was out there, girls were dying, and they were cautious and went out in groups and changed their hair color."

—NYPD detective James Justus

GLOSSARY

amicable
Friendly; showing kindness or goodwill.

arsonist
A person who sets a fire intentionally, committing the crime of arson.

blue-collar
Working-class, usually used to describe a person who performs skilled or unskilled manual labor.

conniving
Inspired to do something immoral, wrong, or illegal.

degradation
Deterioration or decline.

egregious
Extraordinarily shocking and bad.

foreboding
Seeming like something terrible is about to happen.

homicide
When one person kills another person.

monotony
The same thing over and over; a lack of variety that often leads to boredom.

premeditated
Planned or thought out beforehand.

pyromania
Having a love for setting fires and believing that fires hold divine value.

ADDITIONAL RESOURCES

SELECTED BIBLIOGRAPHY

Drell, Cady. "How Son of Sam Changed America." *Rolling Stone*, 29 July 2016, rollingstone.com. Accessed 23 July 2019.

Fishman, Steve. "The Devil in David Berkowitz." *New York*, 8 Sept. 2006, nymag.com. Accessed 27 Apr. 2019.

"Son of Sam: The Killer Speaks." *CBS News*, 11 Aug. 2017, cbsnews.com. Accessed 27 Apr. 2019.

FURTHER READINGS

Carmichael, L. E. *Forensic Science: In Pursuit of Justice*. Abdo, 2015.

Mooney, Carla. *The Zodiac Killer*. Abdo, 2020.

New York Times Editorial Staff. *Serial Killers: Jack the Ripper, Son of Sam and Others*. New York Times Educational Publishing, 2019.

ONLINE RESOURCES

To learn more about the Son of Sam killings, please visit **abdobooklinks.com** or scan this QR code. These links are routinely monitored and updated to provide the most current information available.

MORE INFORMATION

For more information on this subject, contact or visit the following organizations:

ALCATRAZ EAST CRIME MUSEUM

2757 Parkway
Pigeon Forge, TN 37863
865-453-3278
alcatrazeast.com

Explore American history from a different perspective in five galleries that highlight aspects of the US justice and penal systems, explain how forensic science works, reflect on victims' stories and criminals' profiles, and discuss the relationship between crime prevention and law enforcement. Built to resemble a prison, the museum is 25,000 square feet, spread over two floors, and includes more than 100 interactive exhibits.

MUSEUM OF DEATH

6031 Hollywood Blvd.
Hollywood, CA 90028
323-466-8011
museumofdeath.net

The Museum of Death houses the world's largest collection of serial killer artwork, mortician and coroner instruments, Manson Family memorabilia, crime scene photographs, and more. There are two locations, one in Hollywood and the other in New Orleans, Louisiana. Each museum offers a 45-minute self-guided tour of the exhibits and a gift shop.

SOURCE NOTES

CHAPTER 1. SHOTS IN THE DARK

1. "Son of Sam: The Killer Speaks." *CBS News*, 11 Aug. 2017, cbsnews.com. Accessed 8 Aug. 2019.

2. Mary Murphy. "Mother of Son of Sam's First Victim, Donna Lauria, Shares Anguish on 40th Anniversary of Murder." *PIX11*, 30 July 2016, pix11.com. Accessed 8 Aug. 2019.

3. Jerry Oppenheimer. "Son of Sam Survivor Breaks Her Silence after 40 Years." *New York Post*, 17 July 2016, nypost.com. Accessed 8 Aug. 2019.

4. Ed Scarpo. "Son of Sam's First Shooting Suspected to Be a Mob Hit." *Cosa Nostra News*, 13 Aug. 2017, cosanostranews.com. Accessed 8 Aug. 2019.

5. Cristen Conger. "How Police Sketches Work." *How Stuff Works*, n.d., people.howstuffworks.com. Accessed 8 Aug. 2019.

6. Sal Bono. "40 Years after 'Son of Sam' Arrest, Detective Reveals How Cops Finally Ended His Reign of Terror." *Inside Edition*, 1 Aug. 2017, insideedition.com. Accessed 8 Aug. 2019.

7. "This Day in History: August 10. Son of Sam Serial Killer Is Arrested." *History*, 9 Feb. 2010, history.com. Accessed 8 Aug. 2019.

8. Robert D. McFadden. "Profiles of Psychopath's Victims." *New York Times*, 28 June 1977, nytimes.com. Accessed 8 Aug. 2019.

CHAPTER 2. A TROUBLED PAST

1. "The Devil in David Berkowitz." *New York Magazine*, 8 Sept. 2006, nymag.com. Accessed 8 Aug. 2019.

2. Lawrence Klausner. *Son of Sam: Based on the Authorized Transcription of the Tapes, Official Documents, and Diaries of David Berkowitz*. Simon and Schuster, 2017.

3. "The Shocking Reason Serial Killer David Berkowitz Targeted Women." *A&E*, 11 Oct. 2017, aetv.com. Accessed 8 Aug. 2019.

4. "The Devil in David Berkowitz."

5. Klausner, *Son of Sam*.

6. Klausner, *Son of Sam*.

7. Klausner, *Son of Sam*.

8. Scott Bonn. "5 Myths about Serial Killers and Why They Persist [Excerpt]." *Scientific American*, 24 Oct. 2014, scientificamerican.com. Accessed 8 Aug. 2019.

9. Bonn, "5 Myths about Serial Killers."

10. Nathan Laliberte. "Son of Sam: David Berkowitz's History in Westchester County." *Westchester Magazine*, 17 Apr. 2012, westchestermagazine.com. Accessed 8 Aug. 2019.

11. Laliberte, "Son of Sam."

CHAPTER 3. THE SUMMER OF SAM

1. Albert Davila and Mark Liff. "Son of Sam Shoots and Kills Couple Sitting in Parked Car in the Bronx." *New York Daily News*, 17 Apr. 2017, nydailynews.com. Accessed 8 Aug. 2019.

2. William Federici and Paul Meskil. "Son of Sam Leaves Note in Victims' Car Taunting, 'I'll Do It Again.'" *New York Daily News*, 18 Apr. 2017, nydailynews.com. Accessed 8 Aug. 2019.

3. Federici and Meskil, "Son of Sam Leaves Note."

4. Federici and Meskil, "Son of Sam Leaves Note."

5. "David Berkowitz, Son of Sam Killer." *Crime Museum*, n.d., crimemuseum.org. Accessed 8 Aug. 2019.

6. "Son of Sam: The Killer Speaks." *CBS News*, 11 Aug. 2017, cbsnews.com. Accessed 8 Aug. 2019.

7. Jen Carlson. "Watch New Yorkers Talk About 'Son of Sam' Fears in 1977." *Gothamist*, 26 July 2017, gothamist.com. Accessed 8 Aug. 2019.

8. Carlson, "Watch New Yorkers Talk About 'Son of Sam' Fears in 1977."

9. Richard Edmonds and Paul Meskil. "Son of Sam Wounds Couple Near Queens Discotheque." *New York Daily News*, 26 June 2017, nydailynews.com. Accessed 8 Aug. 2019.

10. Saif Choudhury. "Hot Blast from NYC's Past—A History of City's Heat Waves." *Adapt NY*, 27 July 2016, adaptny.org. Accessed 8 Aug. 2019.

11. Sewell Chan. "Remembering the '77 Blackout." *New York Times*, 9 July 2017, nytimes.com. Accessed 8 Aug. 2019.

12. Robert D. McFadden. ".44 Killer Wounds 12th and 13th Victims." *New York Times*, 1 Aug. 1977, nytimes.com. Accessed 8 Aug. 2019.

13. Cacilia Davis. "Key Witness Describes Spotting Son of Sam before Attack." *New York Daily News*, 3 Aug. 2017, nydailynews.com. Accessed 8 Aug. 2019.

14. James Barron. "How a Son of Sam Detective Realized 'This Has Got to Be the Guy.'" *New York Times*, 6 Aug. 2017, nytimes.com. Accessed 8 Aug. 2019.

CHAPTER 4. CAPTURED

1. Richard Edmonds, Lou Parajos, and Paul Meskil. "Son of Sam Victim, 20-Year-Old Stacy Moskowitz, Dies From Gunshot Wounds." *New York Daily News*, 31 July 2017, nydailynews.com. Accessed 8 Aug. 2019.

2. Olivia B. Waxman. "The Letters That Left New Yorkers Terrified of the 'Son of Sam.'" *Time*, 10 Aug. 2017, time.com. Accessed 8 Aug. 2019.

3. Edmonds, Parajos, and Meskil. "Son of Sam Victim."

4. Waxman, "The Letters That Left New Yorkers Terrified of the 'Son of Sam.'"

5. Robert D. McFadden. "Suspect in 'Son of Sam' Murders Arrested in Yonkers; Police Say .44 Caliber Weapon Is Recovered." *New York Times*, 11 Aug. 1977, nytimes.com. Accessed 8 Aug. 2019.

6. McFadden, "Suspect in 'Son of Sam' Murders Arrested."

7. McFadden, "Suspect in 'Son of Sam' Murders Arrested."

8. Robert D. McFadden. "'Sam' Suspect, Heavily Guarded, Arraigned and Held for Testing." *New York Times*, 12 Aug. 1977, nytimes.com. Accessed 8 Aug. 2019.

9. John Hockenberry. "Did 'Son of Sam' Really Act Alone?" *Dateline*, 2 July 2004, nbcnews.com. Accessed 8 Aug. 2019.

10. Waxman, "The Letters That Left New Yorkers Terrified of the 'Son of Sam.'"

11. Hockenberry, "Did 'Son of Sam' Really Act Alone?"

12. Jonathan Wolfe. "New York Today: Son of Sam, 40 Years Later." *New York Times*, 28 July 2017, nytimes.com. Accessed 8 Aug. 2019.

13. Robert Lane and Paul Meskil. "David Berkowitz Is Sentenced to 25 Years to Life in Prison for Son of Sam Killings." *New York Daily News*, 11 June 2015, nydailynews.com. Accessed 8 Aug. 2019.

14. Lane and Meskil, "David Berkowitz Is Sentenced."

15. Lane and Meskil, "David Berkowitz Is Sentenced."

16. "The Letters of Son of Sam." *New York Magazine*, 8 Sept. 2006, nymag.com. Accessed 8 Aug. 2019.

17. David Abrahamsen. "Unmasking Son of Sam's Demons." *New York Times*, 1 July 1979, nytimes.com. Accessed 21 Aug. 2019.

SOURCE NOTES CONTINUED

CHAPTER 5. THE EVIDENCE

1. Ariana Brockington. "How One Mind-Blowingly Simple Mistake Stopped Ted Bundy." *Refinery 29*, 3 May 2019, refinery29.com. Accessed 8 Aug. 2019.

2. Olivia B. Waxman. "How Police Caught Jeffrey Dahmer." *Time*, 22 July 2016, time.com. Accessed 8 Aug. 2019.

3. Chris Harris. "Will Advancements in DNA and Genealogy Help Catch California's Infamous Zodiac Killer?" *People*, 25 Jan. 2019, people.com. Accessed 8 Aug. 2019.

4. Bruce Weber. "Timothy Dowd, Detective Who Led Son of Sam Manhunt, Dies at 99." *New York Times*, 29 Dec. 2014, nytimes.com. Accessed 8 Aug. 2019.

5. Weber, "Timothy Dowd, Detective Who Led Son of Sam Manhunt, Dies at 99."

6. John Hockenberry. "Did 'Son of Sam' Really Act Alone?" *Dateline*, 2 July 2004, nbcnews.com. Accessed 8 Aug. 2019.

7. Lily Rothman. "How the Son of Sam Serial Killer Was Finally Caught." *Time*, 19 Aug. 2015, time.com. Accessed 8 Aug. 2019.

8. Benjamin H. Smith. "10 Serial Killers That Left Disturbing Calling Cards at Their Crime Scenes." *Oxygen*, 6 Feb. 2019, oxygen.com. Accessed 8 Aug. 2019.

9. Zachary Crockett. "What Data on 3,000 Murderers and 10,000 Victims Tells Us about Serial Killers." *Vox*, 2 Dec. 2016, vox.com. Accessed 8 Aug. 2019.

10. "40 Years after 'Son of Sam' Arrest, Detective Reveals How Cops Finally Ended His Reign of Terror." *WSLS*, 1 Aug. 2017, wsls.com. Accessed 8 Aug. 2019.

11. Richard F. Shepard. "About New York: A .44-Caliber Cloud of Fear." *New York Times*, 4 Aug. 1977, nytimes.com. Accessed 8 Aug. 2019.

12. Shepard, "About New York."

CHAPTER 6. A MEDIA FRENZY

1. Jimmy Breslin. "Breslin to Son of Sam: End Your Torment and Give Yourself up to Me." *New York Daily News*, 7 May 2015, nydailynews.com. Accessed 8 Aug. 2019.

2. Richard Edmonds. "'Son of Sam' Says He Can't Stop Killing in Letter to Daily News Columnist Jimmy Breslin." *New York Daily News*, 2 June 2017, nydailynews.com. Accessed 8 Aug. 2019.

3. Cady Drell. "How Son of Sam Changed America." *Rolling Stone*, 29 July 2016, rollingstone.com. Accessed 8 Aug. 2019.

4. Breslin, "Breslin to Son of Sam."

5. Jonathan Wolfe. "New York Today: Son of Sam, 40 Years Later." *New York Times*, 28 July 2017, nytimes.com. Accessed 8 Aug. 2019.

6. Drell, "How Son of Sam Changed America."

7. Chet Flippo. "Steve Dunleavy: The Writer They Call Mr. Blood and Guts." *Rolling Stone*, 19 Apr. 1979, rollingstone.com. Accessed 8 Aug. 2019.

8. Drell, "How Son of Sam Changed America."

9. Drell, "How Son of Sam Changed America."

10. Drell, "How Son of Sam Changed America."

11. David C. Berliner. "Neighbors Recall Quiet Man, a Little Strange, but Nice." *Washington Post*, 12 Aug. 1977, washingtonpost.com. Accessed 8 Aug. 2019.

12. Drell, "How Son of Sam Changed America."

13. Scott A. Bonn. "'Son of Sam' Serial Killer Explains Why He Was Once 'Evil.'" *Psychology Today*, 10 Feb. 2014, psychologytoday.com. Accessed 8 Aug. 2019.

14. Drell, "How Son of Sam Changed America."

CHAPTER 7. CONSPIRACY THEORIES

1. John Hockenberry. "Did 'Son of Sam' Really Act Alone?" *Dateline*, 2 July 2004, nbcnews.com. Accessed 8 Aug. 2019.

2. "Rock Album by Hendrix Is Examined for a Clue On 'Son of Sam's' Name." *New York Times*, 7 July 1977, nytimes.com. Accessed 8 Aug. 2019.

3. Steve Fishman. "The Devil in David Berkowitz." *New York Magazine*, 8 Sept. 2006, nymag.com. Accessed 8 Aug. 2019.

4. Hockenberry, "Did 'Son of Sam' Really Act Alone?"

5. Hockenberry, "Did 'Son of Sam' Really Act Alone?"

6. Hockenberry, "Did 'Son of Sam' Really Act Alone?"

7. Hockenberry, "Did 'Son of Sam' Really Act Alone?"

8. Anthony D'Alessandro. "Son of Sam 40 Years Later: Criminologist Says 'I Don't Believe David Berkowitz Is a Psychopath.'" *Deadline*, 26 July 2017, deadline.com. Accessed 8 Aug. 2019.

9. "Son of Sam: The Killer Speaks." *CBS News*, 11 Aug. 2017, cbsnews.com. Accessed 8 Aug. 2019.

CHAPTER 8. BERKOWITZ'S LEGACY

1. "Son of Sam: The Killer Speaks." *CBS News*, 11 Aug. 2017, cbsnews.com. Accessed 8 Aug. 2019.

2. "Son of Sam Survivor Speaks Out for the First Time 40 Years after Killer Set Out on Murderous Rampage in New York." *Daily Mail*, 17 July 2016, dailymail.co.uk. Accessed 8 Aug. 2019.

3. Sal Bono. "How 'Son of Sam' David Berkowitz Went From Following the Devil to God." *Inside Edition*, 2 Aug. 2017, insideedition.com. Accessed 8 Aug. 2019.

4. Jamie Schram and Natalie Musumeci. "Son of Sam: I've Found My Life's Calling." *New York Post*, 22 June 2016, nypost.com. Accessed 8 Aug. 2019.

5. "Shawangunk Correctional Facility." *PrisonPro*, n.d., prisonpro.com. Accessed 8 Aug. 2019.

6. Julie Beck. "The Grisly, All-American Appeal of Serial Killers." *Atlantic*, 21 Oct. 2014, theatlantic.com. Accessed 8 Aug. 2019.

7. Mary Vespa. "Jimmy Breslin Co-Authors a Son of Sam Novel That's Under Arrest, Saleswise." *People*, 10 July 1978, people.com. Accessed 8 Aug. 2019.

8. Sandra L. Thomas. "Son of Sam Laws." *First Amendment Encyclopedia*, n.d., mtsu.edu. Accessed 8 Aug. 2019.

9. Mary Elizabeth Williams. "Son of Sam Pleads His Case for Parole: 'I've Done a Lot of Good and Positive Things.'" *Salon*, 23 June 2016, salon.com. Accessed 8 Aug. 2019.

10. Jeff Truesdell and Chris Harris. "Inside Son of Sam's Life Now: Born-Again as the 'Son of Hope' and He Doesn't Want to Leave Prison." *People*, 26 July 2017, people.com. Accessed 8 Aug. 2019.

11. Steve Fishman. "The Devil in David Berkowitz." *New York Magazine*, 8 Sept. 2006, nymag.com. Accessed 8 Aug 2019.

12. Paul LaRosa. "Daughter of Man Terrorized by 'Son of Sam' Now Visits Him in Prison." *CBS News*, 11 Aug. 2017, cbsnews.com. Accessed 8 Aug. 2019.

13. Fishman, "The Devil in David Berkowitz."

14. Tanyanika Samuels. "'Son of Sam' David Berkowitz Speaks to the Daily News, Decries Violence as 'Senseless.'" *New York Daily News*, 10 Aug. 2012, nydailynews.com. Accessed 8 Aug. 2019.

15. Samuels, "'Son of Sam' David Berkowitz Speaks to the Daily News."

INDEX

ABOUT THE AUTHOR

Alexis Burling has written dozens of articles and books for young readers on a variety of topics including current events, famous people, nutrition, fitness, careers, money management, relationships, and cooking. She is also a book critic with reviews of both adult and young adult books, author interviews, and other industry-related articles published in the *New York Times*, *Washington Post*, *San Francisco Chronicle*, and more. Burling lives in Portland, Oregon, with her husband, but she spent 15 years living in New York City.